5-7-73

Daniel Berrigan and
Contemporary Protest Poetry

DANIEL BERRIGAN
AND CONTEMPORARY
PROTEST POETRY

by
Harry J. Cargas

COLLEGE & UNIVERSITY PRESS · *Publishers*

NEW HAVEN, CONN.

MANUFACTURED IN THE UNITED STATES OF AMERICA BY
UNITED PRINTING SERVICES, INC.
NEW HAVEN, CONN.

For
Millie Rieder Cargas
a
good
woman

Acknowledgments

Acknowledgments can seem so cold and formal. This one is not meant in that spirit. Maureen O'Brien Thielemier assisted me in the preparation of this book in countless ways, including the support of her buoyant spirit.

This book would have hardly progressed without the knowledgeable guidance of Dr. Raymond Benoit of the English Department at St. Louis University. He is a teacher who knows.

My wife Millie, to whom this book is dedicated, has not only shared in the creation and frustration involved herein, she has shared all of the other moments too—this is her book.

And I want to render a remark of particular respect to Dan Berrigan for being Dan Berrigan.

Thanks are also due to the following for allowing me to quote from the works indicated: Oxford University Press for passages from *Collected Poems 1930-1960*, by Richard Eberhart (1960). Random House, Inc. for permission to quote from the following by Karl Shapiro: "Scyros," "Auto Wreck," "Satire: Anxiety," from *Poems 1940-1953* (1953); "Recapitulations," "The Conscientious Objector," "The Progress of Faust," from *Trial of a Poet* (1947); *In Defense of Ignorance* (1965). Excerpts from *Lord Weary's Castle* by Robert Lowell are reprinted by permission of Harcourt Brace Jovanovich, Inc.; copyright 1944, 1946, by Robert Lowell. City Lights Books for excerpts from *Kaddish and other Poems*, copyright © 1961 by Allen Ginsberg; *Reality Sandwiches*, copyright © 1963 by Allen Ginsberg: *Planet*

Contents

Introduction

THE ALIENATION of the artist from society is an obvious theme. Critics may disagree concerning the causes of this separation—it could be due to greater vision or to unacceptable naivete—but the fact of alienation remains. Currently, the situation is being noticed by an increasing number of citizens, some who do not consider themselves "readers" or "critics" but who know about protesting artists simply from reading newspapers. They find that Pablo Picasso will not attend the opening of a museum built in his honor in Spain because of the government's official attitude toward Basques. Pablo Casals has not been to his native country in decades as a gesture of disapproval of the political environment.

More significant than such headline instances, however, is the work of the artists themselves. There is dissent implicit in much of the disharmony of the classical music being composed now, in painting, the cinema, the novel, and contemporary poetry. It is with this last category that we shall concern ourselves. The point to be made is this: there is an observable trend among certain U.S. poets that indicates a blurring of the distinction between the work written by the poet and the life he lives. We might characterize this as a movement (not organized or consciously directed as through the canons of a "school") toward wholeness. For the authors we shall be examining, art is life and life is art.

I am not qualified to comment on the psychological significance of the tendency toward this wholeness. Students of another discipline will have to analyze this for us. But we shall, here, indicate the trend and comment on its development. The graph, if we plot a chart, leads upward in the direction of increased activism. While Aeschylus in the *Oresteia* dramatized controversial political issues of his times, there is no evidence of his having disturbed his world with the kind of active involvement that was achieved by Daniel Berrigan. Using these two authors as chronological poles, we can list numerous writers who had much to contribute to their contemporary dialogues—and so extreme was their alienation from society that what many of them wrote may have seemed more a monologue than dialogue. Euripides was interesting on women's rights. Aristophanes gibed contemporary political leaders as well as their ideas; Dante was immersed in the political events of his day; and Thomas More was beheaded, drawn, and quartered over a theological-political disagreement. Francis Bacon earned a high government post and used his pen to expound his political beliefs as much as Machiavelli did. John Milton left us *Areopagitica*. James Fenimore Cooper, Harriet Beecher Stowe, Leo Tolstoy, William Butler Yeats, Federico Garcia Lorca, all wrote on political issues because they felt that their art could not be separated from their worldly and fully human concerns.

What these authors have done may be better illuminated by contrasting their life-styles with those of the best known twentieth-century exiles, men like Joyce, Eliot, James, Maugham, Richard Wright, even Ezra Pound. These men left their native countries for a variety of reasons and in so doing eliminated opportunities for serious involvement in true issues. (Pound's work with the Fascists may be viewed as only a superficial participation.)

Both of the above groups may be contrasted with contemporary radicals like Berrigan and LeRoi Jones. While the priest and the black, each a poet-playwright-essayist, are closer to Aeschylus and Dante than to James and Wright, we must notice that they have written and lived in a fashion more closely achieving the kind of wholeness, mentioned earlier, than any of the above. This is true even when we think of More who might be called a "passive activist." While he lived (and therefore died) for his beliefs, he "wrote" these beliefs remarkably little.

We are pointing to two basic approaches to creativity, those explored by Maurice Beebe in *Ivory Towers and Sacred Founts* (New York, 1964). Those who subscribe to the "ivory tower" thesis of creativity believe that an artist must withdraw from life to preserve his creative powers. Opposed to that position are those who find the creativity of the artist rooted in experience in the "real world." The dangers for the artist of accepting the absolute theories of either of these two "schools" are apparent: one can get out of touch with men or one can risk expending all of one's energies in efforts that are not directly related to one's art. No doubt all serious artists consider these poles in regard to the practice of their craft. However as we study Jones and Berrigan and Ginsberg, we begin to understand that a distinction is being erased for these men and others because they cannot accept the notion that their work is separate from their lives. Poetry is not more or less important than participation. Poetry is participation just as participation is poetry.

Art critic John Canaday has said that contemporary painters are "always making desperate effort to relate art to things like Vietnam but all they turn out is a bunch of lousy paintings." His lament is only partially valid because it is too general. Artists, of whatever form, look at Vietnam or other issues and comment on them in their works and in their humanity. We may be witnessing a true revolution in art, one that refuses to accept certain canonized distinctions. When he defined art, Thomas Aquinas stressed the difference between the decorative and useful arts. Daniel Berrigan sees no such difference. To Father Berrigan, a protest poem, while fully poem, can be fully "useful" just as his demonstration at Catonsville, Maryland, in burning draft records, while useful to his goals, was also a fully creative, poetic act.

Whether this is symptomatic of a new understanding of the psychological search for wholeness or not, it is impossible to estimate now. How much of it is in reaction to whatever effect the New Criticism has had on the creative mind it might be entertaining to speculate—but it would certainly be inconclusive. However, the phenomenon is there. Let us examine it.

Note: The subject of Chapter V has adopted the name Imamu Amiri Baraka. There is no attempt here to be disrespectful of this choice. However, since all of the works discussed in Chapter V were published in book form under the name LeRoi Jones it was thought more fitting to make use of the Jones name in this volume.

Daniel Berrigan and
Contemporary Protest Poetry

I

Richard Eberhart: Will Poetry
and Psyche Poetry

IT MAY BE FITTING to begin this discussion of contemporary protest poetry with Richard Eberhart, an artist whose work speaks to the senselessness of war in the greater context of the absurdity of death. Eberhart is not immediately considered a "protest poet," certainly not when compared with Berrigan, LeRoi Jones, or Ginsberg. However if we are to build a pyramid representing the direction our investigation will take (with Berrigan at the top) Eberhart's would appropriately be one of the names at the base of this pyramid. Others would include Stanley Kunitz and Theodore Roethke, for example.[1]

Eberhart was born in Austin, Minnesota, in 1904. He attended the University of Minnesota for a time but achieved his B.A. degree from Dartmouth in 1926. At eighteen, Eberhart had "intimately witnessed: the death of his mother from cancer—a suffering nine month process." After Dartmouth, Eberhart worked as a steamer hand on a ship to the Orient, then enrolled at St. John's College, Cambridge, where he earned an M.A. While there, he studied under F. R. Leavis and I. A. Richards.

The year after graduation, Eberhart's first book was published, *A Bravery of Earth* (1930). During this same year he was tutoring the son of Siam's King Prajadhipok.

From 1933-1941 Eberhart taught at St. Mark's School in Southboro, Massachusetts, where one of his students was Robert Lowell. Eberhart was a naval gunnery officer during World War II after which he has primarily taught although he did devote some time to what is generally referred to as "the business world." In 1956 he joined the faculty at Dartmouth. He has been a Consultant in Poetry at the Library of Congress and he was awarded the Bollingen Prize for *Collected Poems, 1930-1960.*

Perhaps the two most significant experiences for Eberhart, at least for the purposes of this study, were the death of his mother and his military service.

To focus on his war poems is to realize what Babette Deutsch has seen: "His war poems, lyrical in spite of their fierce concision, speak concretely and eloquently of the incongruousness of the concepts of man and of war."[2] In an interview granted after Deutsch's comment was printed, Eberhart supported her concept of the incongruity in his work when he told an interviewer: "I was an aerial machine gunnery instructor in World War II and taught thousands of our young men to shoot out of aircraft at the enemy. I volunteered to service because I believed in my country, but I always had a sense that the conscientious objectors who didn't wear the uniforms had a deeper understanding of man than I did condoning killing by belonging to the war, you see."[3]

Eberhart illustrates the feelings here expressed in his poem "Protagonists."[4] For three stanzas he tells of men who were either killed in the war or came home as heroes. His tone is neither eulogistic nor ironic. In the final five lines, however, the poet indicates his respect for the conscientious objector:

> But I see a man in blue denim, walking
> Through the halls of conscientious objection,
> Because he took Christ seriously, immured.
> A literalist of the imagination! who
> Believed do unto others—Thou shalt not kill!

Eberhart does not write many poems about the person who refuses to kill for moral reasons (the kind of person E. E. Cummings had celebrated as a "conscientious object-/ or" some years earlier). Eberhart, rather, shows us the honors of war. For example, "Protagonists" begins "To the man with his jaw shot away, blood-badged/ As he falls out of the sky to earth or sea,/ Existence is lethal, and then it is not." In "World War" (*CP* p. 96) we read,

> Baby Red Breasted Chained Nippled,
> Pavement Clattering People Crippled,
> Youth Courageous Finger Felled,
> Nutty Manhood Maggot Shelled.

This poem is completed with three lines ending with "World" and a final line finishing with a word indicating serious threat to the world:

> Howls the Whirlwind Over the World,
> Tempests Quaking Shake the World,
> The Earthquake Opens Abrupt the World,
> Cold Dreadful Mass Destruction.

The tempo of this last line, contrasted with that of the preceding three, gives an impressive emphasis to Eberhart's meaning.

The best known of Eberhart's war poems is probably "The Fury of Aerial Bombardment" (*CP*, p. 90). It begins in very general, rhetorical terms and ends with a specificity which jars the reader:

> You would think the fury of aerial bombardment
> Would rouse God to relent; the infinite spaces
> Are still silent. He looks on shock-pried faces,
> History, even, does not know what is meant.

> You would feel that after so many centuries
> God would give man to repent; yet he can kill
> As Cain could, but with multitudinous will,
> No farther advanced than in his ancient furies.

Was man made stupid to see his own stupidity?
Is God by definition indifferent, beyond us all?
Is the eternal truth man's fighting soul
Wherein the Beast ravens in its own avidity?

Of Van Wettering I speak, and Averill,
Names on a list, whose faces I do not recall
But they are gone to early death, who late in school
Distinguished the belt feed lever from the
          belt holding pawl.

John Ciardi's comment on this poem is valuable:

> In stanza four the address suddenly changes from a rhetoric
> for abstract-man to an understated elegy for two boys named
> Van Wettering and Averill, boys who sought no universal mean-
> ing but simply distinguished the belt-feed-lever from the belt-
> holding-pawl, and died of their schooling into the anonymities
> of fate. They are not even faces: they are names on a list. The
> only point at which they touch larger significance is that they
> are gone to early death. Thus, they are unknowing heirs to all
> human waste: their death is their one real illustration of the
> universal questions the poem begins with. Yet the implication is
> clear that their death is both man's tragedy and failure. The
> boys are the least of men in one sense, faceless and forgotten;
> yet their deaths accuse all of mankind, the more so that these
> who die are so insignificant.[5]

It is this willingness to "accuse all of mankind" that gives
power to Eberhart's writing. A poem that illustrates this
point is titled "On Shooting Particles Beyond the World"
(*CP*, p. 129). It is about the atomic bomb. Heading the
poem is a newspaper quotation in which an authority is
cited as saying that the end of it all will be the blowing up
of ourselves. The author mocks man's discontent—a frustration that arises from having to limit war to earth. Now man
attempts to send the effects of his sickness to the very
heavens. "Good Boy Man! Your innards are put out,/ From
now all space will be your vomitorium." This is followed
by a verse which reads,

> The atom bomb accepted this world,
> Its hatred of man blew death in his face.
> But not content, he'll send slugs beyond,
> His particles of intellect will spit on the sun.

The final four lines tell us that it is not God who will be found "in the mystery of space"—far from it, as man "flaunts his own out-cast state." Man will instead discover the opposite of God, his own "shout that gives a hissing sound." (Compare this with Stephen Dedalus' notion of God as a shout in the street in *Ulysses*.)

Man, through his invention of mass destructive weapons, is scored in another poem, "Aesthetics after War" (*CP*, p. 122). The poet writes of seeing

> ... man's total malice over Hiroshima,
> That gigantic, surrealistic, picture-mushroom
> And objectification of megalomania.
> A world of men who butcher men
> In the arsenical best interests of several states,
> The modern warring maniacal man.

It is indeed a mad man who perpetrates war. However, it is a madness far removed from that in the poem "If I could only live at the Pitch that is near Madness" (*CP*, p. 53) in which the violence and vividness of childhood become material for nostalgia. Replying to an interviewer's question, Eberhart himself makes the distinction: "It's good to be at the pitch that is near madness. That's when you are nearest to the divine insight. The war experience had fury, but this is the objective fury of destructiveness" (Donoghue, p. 21).

One meaning of war is death and Eberhart emphasizes this meaning. However, his concern with death goes beyond war in his work. We could expect this of a person who, at eighteen, "participated" in the lingering death of his mother. There is no way, of course, to pinpoint how or why the subject of death should attract Eberhart any more than it attracts any other human being. Eberhart is interested in the fascination of death, common to poets. "You will notice that in the history of English poetry there have been more great poems about death than there have been about birth. . . . Isn't it interesting that, for instance, birth is positive, life-giving, death is negative and life-taking-away, and yet death transports the imagination of a poet much more than birth" (Donoghue, pp. 14-15). Philip Booth notes that "Eberhart is repeatedly most incisive when his poems confront death. This 'savage mystery' has been his lifelong concern, and he is most his own poet when, considering mortality, he observes himself as man-in-relation-to-nature."[6] Later, Booth continues, "What death *means*, in Eberhart's poetry, is an inexplicable mystery. Eberhart's great honesty is that his poems confront this mystery on its own terms, reserving for themselves only the equal mystery of life's sweet vitality" (p. 66).

In a work cited earlier, Ralph Mills, Jr., supports these remarks. "In fact," he writes, "'mortality,' 'mentality,' and 'men's actions' may be said to become Eberhart's chief themes throughout his career" (p. 13). Eberhart can use "any excuse" to meditate or speculate on death. It could be the demise of a soldier, a visit to a cemetery, the death of an animal. Some of the titles of his poems will themselves reveal his interest in death. The following are found in *Collected Poems 1930-1960*: "Grave Piece" (p. 48); "I Walked Out to the Graveyard to see the Dead" (p. 53); "I walked over the Grave of Henry James" (p. 60); "Sometimes the Longing for Death" (p. 106); "Birth and Death" (p. 226); and, of course, all of the war poetry. There are others, as well, including two poems which seem particularly to recall certain of Emily Dickinson's poems: "When Golden Flies upon my Carcass Come" (p. 41), and "Imagining How it would be to be Dead" (p. 59). The former title easily reminds us of Miss Dickinson's "I heard a Fly buzz—when I died," while the latter title expresses Dickinson's theme in "Because I could not stop for Death—."

"The Lamb" (*CP*, p. 4) is a poem that uses the death of an animal as a starting point for rumination on death. More familiar in this category, however, is "The Groundhog" (*CP*, p. 23), a poem frequently anthologized. The poem begins in June, the month of life. The narrator is "amid the golden fields" and "in the vigorous summer." Everything bespeaks life and all of a sudden "my senses shook" to be reminded of personal mortality: "Seeing nature ferocious in him." The reaction, then, on seeing the "maggots' might" is one of frustration, hence the poke with the "angry stick." A fearful contrast between life and death dominates the narrator's thought at this point:

> The fever arose, became a flame
> And Vigour circumscribed the skies,
> Immense energy in the sun,
> And through my frame a sunless trembling.

Add to this the frustration of the next line ("My stick had done nor good nor harm") and we can imagine the narrator's rage. The poem's forty-eight lines tell how the narrator found a dead groundhog in June, and of his reaction: "Half with loathing, half with a strange love,/ I poked him with an angry stick." He returns in the autumn and only the "the bony sodden hulk remained." The "sap [had] gone out of the groundhog . . . . And in intellectual chains/ I lost both love and loathing." Another summer saw "only a little hair left." A second stick appears here—but not the angry one of the first summer, instead a "walking stick from a birch." Three years later now, as the story is told, "There is no sign of the groundhog." The narrator considers the meaning of mortality—and consequently of life—in the last four lines:

> And thought of China and of Greece,
> Of Alexander in his tent;
> Of Montaigne in his tower,
> Of St. Theresa in her wild lament.

The speaker does not lose himself in a fury of depression, however. He "kept my reverence for knowledge" and through this the poet arrives at some consolation. This is perhaps the consolation that death and physical corruption are the first steps in growth and evolution. In autumn he returns to the spot of his meditation and finds "The sap gone out of the groundhog," symbolic, no doubt, of the passion for life that has left the narrator:

> But the year had lost its meaning
> And in intellectual chains
> I lost both love and loathing,
> Mured up in the wall of wisdom.

The following summer the narrator returns to find "only a little hair left,/ And bones bleaching in the sunlight/ Beautiful as architecture." He cuts a walking stick. There is far greater acceptance of death here than in his first encounter with the corpse. It takes a final visit, however, for a final statement: "There is no sign of the groundhog." The narrator thinks about this and again presents himself in contrast: "I stood there in the whirling summer,/ My hand capped a withered heart," where summer still stands for life but "withered heart" expresses the awareness of approaching death. This is followed by the four last lines about the dead civilizations of China and Greece, the dead conqueror Alexander, the dead philosopher Montaigne, and finally the dead holy woman Theresa.

The poem is an ambiguous statement. Does the narrator accept death in the end or not? James M. Reid explains the closing a little too facilely when he says that "The poem ends, appropriately, not with serenity but on a note of 'wild lament.' He [the narrator] still does not philosophically accept death."[7] It is not, after all, the narrator's wild lament (much less Eberhart's) that is observed. Certainly there seems to be some acceptance: There is a progression from the first visit to the last. Initially, the narrator reacted to what he saw with shaking senses. On the second visit he is wiser, though less happy than previously. Still later, the beauty of bleached bones is remarked and finally, the narrator can see a universal meaning in the groundhog's death.

It is almost impossible to believe that we are meant to see little change in the narrator as the poem proceeds, except some loss of energy in anger at death. We would misread if one simply substituted "Saint Theresa in her wild lament" for the narrator poking "him with an angry stick." The poem is cast as a series of journeys which are really intellectual journeys, in effect. In each case, a destination is reached, and the point of the inner travels seems to be that each stop (for meditation) is at a point beyond the previous stop.

This interpretation is consistent with other of Eberhart's poems and with comments he has made on death. In "Notes on Poetry" he writes: "Divisive man can know unity only at death (or so he can speculate), and he cannot know what kind of unity that is" (quoted in Mills, pp. 17-18). In a separate essay, Mills has an observation that seems exact and true to the "The Groundhog" as well as other poems:

> A sensitivity to death, to its eruption in the midst of a full existence, haunts Eberhart's poetry and stems, at least partially, from this bitter childhood circumstance (witnessing his mother's death). We never find in the poems a fear of death as such. Sometimes death exerts a spell over the poet's imagination; sometimes it seems merely an intrusion on life or a means of humiliation for man. In some of the visionary poems, Eberhart attempts to project himself beyond the boundaries of life, with differing effects. He has adjusted to the idea of death without succumbing to the sort of obsession with extinction that fills the atmosphere of say, Dylan Thomas's poetry.[8]

Lines from other Eberhart poems will illustrate the meaning of Mills's insights. In "Sometimes the Longing for Death" (*CP*, p. 106), we read of the suggestion of death as "New life, painful no more,/ Where hope does not need to deter us." In "Rumination" there is the hopeful idea that death will "blow his breath/ To fire my clay, when I am still." Death may be regarded as a process of purification in the poem "In a Hard Intellectual Light" (*CP*, p. 28). Yet one more example is found in "Grave Piece" (*CP*, p. 48) where we read "And through Death I try to reach perfection."

While death is an ultimate mystery for Eberhart, it is not the only mystery for him. He stated it rather prosaically to an interviewer when he said simply that "I think poetry is a mysterious business" (Donoghue, p. 8). He does not simply quit with that, however. He has thoughts about poetic creation before the mystery enshrouds. His well-known distinction between "Will poetry" and "Psyche poetry" is to the point: "Psyche poetry pertains to the soul, to peace, quiet, tranquility, serenity, harmony, stillness and silence. It provides psychic states of passive pleasure."[9] (This seems close to the kind of poetry Wordsworth was writing about— and defending—in his "Preface" to the *Lyrical Ballads*.) Eberhart then says that "Will poetry exists because of the power in the cell beyond its energy to maintain itself. Will results in action through wish, zeal, volition, passion, determination, choice, and command. Will makes something happen in poetry."[10] Eberhart nowhere says that he favors one particular type of poetry, will or psyche. He has himself produced outstanding poems of each type. "The Fury of Aerial Bombardment" is his most widely known will poem while "Life as Visionary Spirit" (*CP*, p. 184) best illustrates his psyche poetry. Mills correctly observes that in his psyche poems Eberhart "contemplates sympathetically and dispassionately the nature of life, the function of his art, the full spectrum of experience discussed here under separate and partial thematic headings of perception, death and human behavior." Nevertheless a sensitive reader may believe that Eberhart favors will poetry. What he says of contemplation in "Aesthetics after War" also applies to his poetry:

[26]

> In the East contemplation is self-annihilation,
> In the West it never escapes intrusive action.

It is in the will poetry that Eberhart's "intrusive action" as a poet takes place and it is here that his reputation as a protest poet will be made.

The significance for us here is understood by Mills. While discussing Eberhart's poetry Mills says, "The aesthetic experience does not exist apart from the realities of life."[11] He elaborates further when analyzing the poem "The Goal of Intellectual Man" (*CP*, p. 52) in which the poet sees love as resolution, the "Composing of all human power." Mills writes, "For love, if it is honest and deep, creates distinctions and judgments, rises into anger at the sign of man's failure to be what he can or what he pretends." At this juncture, Eberhart's personal lyricism blends with his public view: "The visionary impulse and the moral grown together" ("Reflections," pp. 92-93). Life "Forces truth upon us" Eberhart declares in "Austere Poem" (*CP*, p. 205). Then he says in fine humility, "I bend to my indeavour," and adds, "May truth breed life."

The internationally respected psychiatrist Joost A. M. Meerloo has found that "Man creates, as it were, out of his mortal wounds."[12] This is perfectly descriptive of the poet whose aesthetic experiences are not separated from life's realities. It is true of Eberhart and true of the poets who are discussed in later sections. It may not be as obvious in Eberhart as it is in, say, LeRoi Jones, but a poem like "Aesthetics after War" supports the point. In it, Eberhart asks "Should a thinking aesthetician want to know God?/ Will God appear in the ultimate stillness of the rose?" It is in this poem, we must remember, that Eberhart cites "man's total malice over Hiroshima," and writes of man's megalomania for war. The first major division of the poem ends: "Is this world of men inimical/ To the postulates of the study aesthetics?" The emphasis, for purposes of our discussion, ought to be on *this world* and *aesthetics*. Eberhart will not find them exclusive terms, but dependent categories. Near the close of this relatively long poem Eberhart writes;

> Is there any doubt that Christ was the most
>   aesthetic man?
> As aestheticism is a part of philosophy,
> Philosophy a part of life,
> Life action, for even the Nirvana-seeker
>   still breathes,
> And Stylites pulls up food in a basket,
> So Christ contemplated the ultimate origin,
> But originated the ultimate rules of action.

Then Eberhart answers the question he posed earlier by saying of the poet, "His blood is in the rose he contemplates" and ends with a tribute to the value of poetry:

> Poetry is so mad and so kind
> It is so majestic an inventive surprise,
> Is it any wonder that in it
> The spirit of man arise?

Notes and References

1. Ralph Mills, Jr., says that Eberhart, Kunitz, and Roethke are "the three senior poets who broke ground for that generation, which also includes Robert Lowell, John Berryman, and Karl Shapiro." See his pamphlet *Richard Eberhart* (Minneapolis, 1966), p. 5.

2. *Poetry in Our Time* (Garden City, New York, 1963), p. 415.

3. Denis Donoghue, "An Interview with Richard Eberhart," *Shenandoah*, XV (Summer, 1964), 20.

4. *Collected Poems* (New York, 1960), p. 181. All subsequent references to Eberhart's poems will be from this edition.

5. John Ciardi, *How Does a Poem Mean?* (Boston, 1959), p. 999.

6. Philip Booth, "The Varieties of Poetic Experience," *Shenandoah*, XV (Summer, 1964), 65.

7. Laurence Perrine and James M. Reid, *100 American Poems of the Twentieth Century* (New York, 1966), p. 194.

8. "Reflections on Richard Eberhart," *Chicago Review*, XV (Summer-Autumn, 1962), 89.

9. Quoted in *ibid.*, p. 34.

10. *Ibid.*, p. 35.

11. *Ibid.*, p. 92.

12. *Suicide and Mass Suicide* (New York, 1968), p. 171.

II

Karl Shapiro: Rebellion as a
Way of Poetry

IT WOULD BE too easy to say that because Karl Shapiro
is Jewish he is a rebel, a writer in protest, in spite of the
fact that Shapiro himself might encourage this kind of
thinking. In an essay titled "The Jewish Writer in America," Shapiro says that "Whatever Jewish consciousness I
possess today I can trace to the writings of the American
Classicists who made it their business to equate 'American'
and 'Jew' as twin evils. This consciousness of myself as
American Jew restricted and narrowed my writing for many
years, erecting a private ghetto in my mind."[1] Further,
Shapiro collected previously published poems in a volume
he called *Poems of a Jew* (New York, 1958) which might
support the idea that the roots of his rebellious posture
were in his Jewishness. He even goes so far as to write a
poem of apparently ultimate humiliation. The narrator in
"The First Time" (p. 28) visits a house of prostitution for
the first time and shows all the nervousness and anxiety we
might imagine. The girl he is to take, who proves to be
younger than he,

> . . . turns round, as one turns at a desk,
> And looks at him, too naked and too soon,
> And almost gently asks: *Are you a Jew?*

We are being asked to feel here that the one who is considered the lowest of society can still look down upon the
Jew.

As one critic points out, however, concerning the publication of *Poems of a Jew*, the theme of Jew as scapegoat simply does not work. Louis Rubin says that in 1958, when the book came out, Shapiro was looking for an absolute, something to replace his sense of lost innocence. This prelapsarian state was lost because as bourgeois poet he came to know too much (more on this later):

> He asks himself, that is, what it is that he can be sure of, and he decides that whatever else he is, he is a Jew, and that this means, in his own words, "a certain state of consciousness which is inescapable." The Jew, whatever else he may or may not be, is someone absolutely committed to this world, who "represents the primitive ego of the human race," and the Jews as a people are "beyond philosophy, beyond art, virtually beyond religion, a stranger even to mysticism . . . at the very center of the divine manifestation—man." Which is another way of saying, I think, that if one thinks of himself in this way he can put aside the search for a cultural system and trust to the concrete cultural identity thus afforded him.[2]

We may suspect that Shapiro uses Jewishness as a lazy way of creating a background. Allen Ginsberg, a poet discussed later, is also Jewish and also a rebel writer. It is not his Jewishness, however, that is credited (or blamed) or exploited. There is at least a hint of this exploitation in Shapiro. It would be absurd to suggest that Shapiro's Jewishness had no effect on his poetic themes. The point to be made is that he neither develops the relationship between Jewishness and rebellion, nor is his Jewishness the exclusive source of his protesting verse.

Karl Jay Shapiro was born in Baltimore, Maryland, in 1913. He attended the University of Virginia and Johns Hopkins University. He first began writing poems in high school—under the influence of an older brother—and after his first year of college began writing very seriously. His first book, *Poems*, was printed in 1935. He was in Australia as a serviceman during World War II and published *The*

Place of Love there in 1942. Two other volumes came out during the war: *Person, Place and Thing* (1942) and a book which won for Shapiro the Pulitzer Prize, *V-Letter and Other Poems* (1944). These two works were edited by Evalyn Katz, Shapiro's fiancée. After the war he was Consultant in Poetry at the Library of Congress and in 1947 began teaching creative writing at Johns Hopkins. Three years later Shapiro became a lecturer at both Loyola and the University of Chicago and became an editor of *Poetry* magazine. His editorship lasted until 1956 when he joined the faculty of the University of Nebraska in the Department of English. He also became editor there of *Prairie Schooner*. Some other books by Shapiro are *Essay on Rime* (1945), *Trial of a Poet and other Poems* (1947), *Poems 1942-1953* (1953), *Poems of a Jew* (1958), *In Defense of Ignorance* (1960), *The Bourgeois Poet* (1964), and *Selected Poems* (1968). This last won a share for Mr. Shapiro, along with John Berryman, of the Bollingen Prize.

It is when writing from his war experience that we here consider Shapiro as protest poet. He writes of the meaninglessness of war in "Scyros,"[3] a poem whose images, according to John Ciardi, are built on paradoxes and whose unpunctuated lines "emphasize that sense of meaninglessness."[4] The poem begins with a man being inducted and a President talking to his military hierarchy. Shapiro writes of "the heaps of shrunken dead," of England and France being lost, "And China staunched her milk and wept for bread." We read of the "Strafing of tulips" from the hands of children (a familiar symbol today) and then the final two stanzas:

> Hot is the sky and green
> Where Germans have been seen
> The moon leaks metal on the Atlantic fields
>   Park boys in birthday shrouds
>   Look lightly through the clouds
> Or Coast the peaks of Finland on their shields

That prophet year by year
Lay still but could not hear
Where scholars tapped to find his new remains
Gog and Magog ate port
In vertical New York
And war began next Monday on the Danes.

The great power of the last line is double: in its matter of factness and in the revelation that it is the peaceful Danes who are, almost as a matter of course, being attacked.

Violence is an integral part of Shapiro's existence. He is aware of growing up, of being annually measured by acts of violence. In his autobiographical "Recapitulations"[5] he informs us that his first decade saw Von Moltke fall (first year), the assassination of Archduke Ferdinand (second year), France in war (age three), and so on through the decade 1914-1924. Perhaps the most pathetic, at least on a personal level, is the couplet recorded after the seventh year:

At eight the boom began to tire,
I tried to set our house on fire.

It seems that the growing youngster was indeed to become a part of his milieu, as destructive as the world in which he was being raised. "What evils do not retrograde/ To my first odious decade?" is the metrically inadequate rhetorical question that ends the poem. For Shapiro, or for the narrator of some of his best war poems, personal involvement in military violence was to be a major theme.

Again in "Recapitulations" we see more autobiography, particularly in the eighth section beginning with, "For four years stupefied by martial law/ The poet in khaki held his tongue." Ironic observations follow this and five sections later he wonders if he should have resisted the war call:

My best friend was in a prison flung.
Tell me, conscience, was I wrong?

In a later poem, "The Conscientious Objector" (*Trial*, p. 38), the question still troubles him. The person who "tells" this poem speaks about a man who goes to jail rather than participate in war, with "The dog authority slavering at your throat." The first stanza ends with "Punishment you felt was clean." Still, the answer is not a clear one as the second line of these final four indicates:

> Yet you who saved neither yourselves nor us
> Are equally with those who shed the blood
> The heroes of our cause. Your conscience is
> What we come back to in the armistice.

This universalizing (pluralizing of) the conscientious objectors being addressed shows an admiration for what sacrifices they had made, but they are only equal to, not superior to, those of the fighting men.

In "Demobilization" (*Trial*, p. 28) it is Shapiro, presumably, who recognizes himself as a "graduate from war." He ironically sees himself in "This is the Class of 'Fortyfive." However, this almost light tone cannot be sustained. The person in "Homecoming" (*Trial*, p. 25) can only seek "forgiveness of the things that thrust/ Shame and all death on millions and on me." This last is not a unique concept in Shapiro's work. In the personal "Recapitulations" he had written of coming back from the war:

> It was the death he never quite forgot
> Through the four years of death, and like as not
> The true death of the best of all of us
> Whose present life is largely posthumous. (p. 9)

However, war in general, apart from personal experience, has also haunted Shapiro. His "Elegy for a Dead Soldier" (*Poems*, p. 42) is an excellent example. Louise Bogan calls it "one of the few war poems worth reading"[6] while Louis Rubin, Jr., has referred to it as "what is probably the finest

poem written about the second world war."[7] The death of
the anonymous soldier is the "the absurd catastrophe,"
something not repeated in other deaths. Each one is an
individual tragedy:

> We ask for no statistics of the killed,
> For nothing political impinges on
> This single casualty, or all those gone,
> Missing or healing, sinking or dispersed
> Hundreds of thousands counted, millions lost.
> More than an accident and less than willed
> Is every fall, and this one like the rest.
> However others calculate the cost,
> To us the final aggregate is *one*,
> One with a name, one transferred to the blest;
> And though another stoops and takes the gun,
> We cannot add the second to the first.

The problem, of course, is in society where "Every
Walden fails" ("Birthday poem," *Poems*, p. 17). Instead,
"We have our wars to quicken us." The result becomes our
insensitivity to violence, where the title object in the "The
Gun" (*Poems*, p. 69) becomes "the toy of my terror," and
where we can read in "Full Moon: New Guinea," of the
"burr," the "tickle" of bombers, illustrating the horror of
war-intoxicated times.

The significance of war for Shapiro is found in a relatively early poem, "The Progress of Faust" (*Trial*, p. 51).
In seven stanzas this work traces the Faust legend from its
inception in Germany "as you would suspect" in the early
sixteenth century to the present. We are reminded of
Marlowe's play in which Faust is associated with Francis
Bacon; we see him in the French Revolution and in his
return to Germany through Goethe and later the Third
Reich. However, most staggering for us is his appearance six
years after the advent of World War II. It is in the Ameri-
cans that Faust has currently settled in what Laurence Perrine has called a "brilliant poem":[8]

> Five years unknown to enemy and friend
> He hid, appearing on the sixth to pose
> In an American desert at war's end
> Where, at his back, a dome of atoms rose.

It will be seen that war is not the only kind of violence that has a kind of terrorizing fascination for Shapiro in his poetry. There is the "war within a war" (*Trial*, p. 14) in "Recapitulations." Here Shapiro observes,

> The black men of our land
> Were seen to walk with pure white girls
>   Laughing and hand in hand
> This most unreasonable state
> No feeling White would tolerate.

Nor is this taken seriously, unfortunately:

> But though a certain number died
> You would not call it fratricide.

(In another poem, "Conscription Camp" [*Poems*, p. 30], Shapiro tells the state of Virginia that "The black man is your conscience and your cost.") "Auto Wreck" (*Poems*, p. 13) points to another kind of violence—even more unreasonable than war or racial strife:

> For death in war is done by hands;
> Suicide has cause and stillbirth, logic;
> And cancer, simple as a flower, blooms.
> But this invites the occult mind,
> Cancels our physics with a sneer

The imagery in this poem is most effective. The narrator sees the ambulance speeding:

> Its quick soft silver bell beating, beating,
> And down the dark one ruby flare
> Pulsing out red light like an artery . . .

The police arrive and, as the ambulance pulls away with the "mangled," do their duty:

> One is still making notes under the light
> One with a bucket douches ponds of blood
> Into the street and gutter.
> One hangs lanterns on the wrecks that cling,
> Empty husks of locusts, to iron poles.

Shapiro can write of the violence of death, as in "Hill at Parramatta" (*Poems*, p. 71), or the natural violence of the rich as in "Satire: Anxiety" (*Poems*, p. 125) wherein

> . . . men of wiser blood and bone
> Destroying me for the things they own—
> Their taxes, vital tubes, and sons
> Submissive in a world of guns.

Yet it is a kind of holy violence, I suspect, that Shapiro himself attempts to perpetrate in his iconoclasm. This is seen in his poems (particularly in their form) but primarily in his criticism.

A poem like "The Fly" (*Poems*, p. 56) is meant to offend. "O hideous little bat, the size of snot," is line one. It is an apostrophe to one who will "inlay maggots like a jewel." The narrator says that as a man he "Must mangle with my shoe and smear your blood, / Expose you your little guts pasty and white." It has been properly said of this poem that "It will perhaps never be chanted at a ladies' club luncheon."[9] But another critic has noted more significantly that "the miracle of the fly's organism, the pathos of its small existence, as well as its ugliness and uselessness or worse from the human viewpoint, make for the poem's complexity."[10]

The poetic use of the ordinary recalls the work of William Carlos Williams. Sam Bradley points out Shapiro's admiration for Williams.[11] It is sufficient to remember the Williams who introduced Allen Ginsberg's early poems,

Empty Mirror. Williams encourages here the poeticizing "of human beings in all the stages of the day, the trip to the bathroom, to the stairs of the subway, the steps of the office or factory routine ... " p. 5). This affiliation of thought will make Shapiro seem vulgar, a rebel of poetic material, and this judgment would not be unfair. If Eberhart wants poetry to reflect life, Shapiro (and Ginsberg and LeRoi Jones) wants it to reflect any aspect of life he chooses under his own adopted heading of bourgeois poet.

What we have in Shapiro is a rebel. This is obvious in many of his writings, particularly his prose. He prides himself in being anti-intellectual. "You will recognize that the position I take is that of the anti-intellectual, as sorry as the name may sound" (*Ignorance*, p. 6). This is found in a book of essays which is preceded by one page which contains only the following words:

> everything
> we are taught
> is false

Much space in this volume is given to attacking the intellectuality of T. S. Eliot and Ezra Pound.[12] Elsewhere Shapiro insists that the poet "be rescued from the world of Culture and the world of History ..."[13] Shapiro himself perhaps gives the best interpretation of the significance of his words in a lecture delivered at Carleton College in 1964:[14]

> I was in an art gallery and heard two curators discussing a large new canvas with paint in some places an inch thick. They were discussing the cost of saving this new painting which the artist had painted in such a way that it would disintegrate in a year or so. That was the artist's intention and he was right. But culture was out to trick him. Culture is always out to trick the artist into immortality and permanence. Ninety-nine times out of a hundred it succeeds. It is the hundredth artist—the one who escapes culture, who serves the world best. He serves the world by entering it and leaving it. If you follow my observa-

tions about the fates of poems and poets, you will see that I am propounding the survival of the artist as a man, not as a divinity or an oracle.

This is supported by another comment by Shapiro in "The Unemployed Magician": "Poetry is humanizing, not civilizing. It allows men to survive in the only world they know—the world of themselves" (*Ignorance*, p. 259). Shapiro's attitude on the subject is best revealed in the sentences which immediately follow:

> Not outside the law but in spite of it. Why is the lawbreaker or the man of passion a hero? Because in him the drama of the human predicament comes to life. Why is Odysseus a hero? Because he is both loyal and treacherous. Why is Oedipus a hero? Because he committed instinctively the most terrible crime against nature. Why is Hamlet a hero? Because he is weak in his nobility. Every schoolboy knows Milton's sympathy for Satan, that prince of exiles upon whom you model yourself. But the perfect man or the perfect devil puts you to sleep. He has no reality, no presence.

All of this leads one to believe that Karl Shapiro is simply trying too hard, possibly too consciously, to rebel. In one place he writes that "The artist's contribution to religion must be in the nature of things heretical." This is in his Introduction to *Poems of a Jew* (p. 28) which tried to establish *Jew*, in all its shock value, with rebel value. To repeat, it does not work. Shapiro finds it necessary to render a note which tells about two of his poems, and what his "shocking" is intended to do: "Freud speaks (it may be all too often) of 'violent defloration' and 'the fear of being eaten by the Father.' In Freud's view, as in that of every Jew, mutilation, circumcision, and 'the fear of being eaten' are all one. *The Leg* is a poem written during war and its subject is the wholeness even of the mutilated. The poem *Mongolian Idiot* has the same theme" (*Jew*, p. 70).

Addressing himself to this point, Richard Slotkin says;

"It is in particular poems like 'Mongolian Idiot,' that Shapiro comes closest to articulating his concept of Judaism in positive, dramatically realized terms. The mother of the 'monster' (and the Jewish community in general, according to the law which Shapiro cites outside the poem) accepts the idiot too as a thing of God, as part of that shocking intimacy between the Jew, the man and the God that His World reveals."[15]

Yet there is an inconsistency in Shapiro indicating that what Slotkin observes is an exception. We cannot doubt the sincerity of Shapiro's efforts toward rebellion, toward heresy, in the direction of iconoclasm. We only have to look at his prose poems, like "The Dirty Word" (*Poems*, p. 35), to see that. Furthermore, his explanation of why this was his favorite poem, at least at one point in his career, is interesting:

> I wrote "The Dirty Word" almost twenty years ago and others in the same vein, yet it has taken me a lifetime to wear this form like my own coat. In those days I was just trying it on. Now I feel ashamed when I write meter and rhyme, or dirty, as if I were wearing a dress. . . .
>
> The dirty word is a kind of sacred mystery. That's what the poem is saying. It should not be let out of the cage, as unfortunately it has been. It should not be domesticated. Nowadays the poor dirty word is dying of popcorn.[16]

(This may bring to mind Graham Greene's story "The Innocent"[17] which is about the "purity, the intensity, the pain of that passion" of not a nasty word but an obscene picture drawn in childhood but looked at thirty years later.)

The inconsistencies, however, if we are to look at Shapiro's work in some depth, remain, His anti-intellectualism either diminishes or is symbolic only. Anthony Ostroff calls Shapiro "King of the Beats,"[18] but Rubin (p. 16) also noticed that in "A Malebolge of 1400 Books" Shapiro "shows signs of backtracking in his attitude toward

Eliot and Pound." Earlier in Rubin's article we are reminded that in an essay titled "What is Anti-Criticism?"
Shapiro reverses himself, "and while he was at it he went
all the way: he defended the New Criticism, he defended
Culture Poetry, and he attacked all those who were against
it" (p. 10). Rubin follows this with what I consider particularly damning words: "Why did Shapiro do this? Again I
think the answer is to be found not in his cultural or
literary convictions, but in his poetry. The kind of poetry
Shapiro defended (and in so doing, explained) was the kind
of poetry he was attempting to write at the time." Edwin
Fussell saw something significant on this point in Shapiro's
early work. In discussing the title poem of *Trial of a Poet*
Fussell says; "Appalled by the violence and dishonesty of
the assaults then made on modern poetry, criticism, and
thought, Shapiro was evidently already swinging away from
the incipient anti-intellectualism which had tempted him in
Essay on Rime (1945)."[19]

Shapiro may shout in *The Bourgeois Poet* "The opposite
enthralls me"; he may insist that "I prefer the poetry of
the commonplace to that of the dream"; he may write with
the trace of a sneer that "Modern poetry claims a moral
prerogative in the name of culture. It is this Culture which
is the substitute for religion and which is the cement of
Modern Poetry," but it is not enough. His performance
does not permit it to be. What he damns in Ezra Pound,
Shapiro praises in Dylan Thomas as "bravado" (see *Ignorance*, pp. 171-186, especially p. 181). The inconsistency
damages Shapiro's credentials as a serious thinker.

"Poetry is innocent, not wise. It does not learn from
experience, because each poetic experience is unique"
(*Primer*, p. 23). Shapiro's words here fascinate for a while
but they do not seem to mean anything. Surely his own
poetry evolves as he himself does. We may say this of his
form but more particularly of his meaning—this despite
what one critic of Shapiro's work has noticed as the poet's

"persistent irritation with *explication de texte* and a steady scholarly interest in prosody" (Fussell, p. 235).

One explanation of the direction Shapiro's development has taken may be seen as a result of the growing distance in time from his military experience. Rubin is correct when he says,

> Whatever the personal discomforts of serving in the Pacific, it should be noted that so far as his status and reputation as a poet were concerned, Shapiro's military service conferred at least two distinct advantages. For one thing, it isolated him from the American literary establishment, allowing his reputation to grow and flourish without his getting involved in whatever politics, personalities and the like go along with making one's professional way in the hierarchy. More importantly, at a time when in technique and status both he was moving from strength to strength, it kept him in a situation whereby he remained an "amateur" rather than a "professional" poet. By this I mean that in the army his experience was of necessity primarily non-intellectual and non-literary, was shared by millions of others who were in no way intellectuals and military men, and thus did not cut him off from what as a poet was peculiarly the source of his strength—his ability to give form and meaning to common, everyday experience. (p. 4)

However, Shapiro is further from this "denominating" experience as time goes on and his work shows it. He may say he prefers the poetry of the commonplace; he may delight in saying of one of his own books (*The Bourgeois Poet*) that "Much of the poem is phony (bourgeois), in bad faith, or even phony-bourgeois. It is not elevated to a style. Sometimes it must display the staggering banality of institutionalized life itself."[20] Shapiro's mere words are not proof enough that he continues to be of the same philosophical persuasion he always was. I am not faulting him for this, but he should be faulted if he fails to recognize it. Perhaps he is aware of a certain inconsistency, however. In reevaluating the work of Pound he said, "I am not concerned about making these remarks consistent with any I have made in the past—in the event that anyone should go to the trouble of comparing them" (quoted in Rubin, p. 16).

What we ultimately have, in our development of the contemporary protest poet, is one who rebels against himself. Perhaps this is the necessary logical final product of literary rebellion—or indeed any rebellion. One fears to become part of the establishment; so as one sees his own position possibly being accepted, becoming indeed the establishment position, he must necessarily (if committed to the philosophy of rebelliousness) turn against his own former stance.

Here is the position in which Karl Shapiro may finally find himself. It may be through the logic of thoughtful choice as I suggest. It may perhaps be through some confusion of intentions or execution. Future critics will be able to solve that puzzle better from a different persepctive in time. Suffice it for our purposes to say that Shapiro may indeed be a model for the ultimate in protest poetry.

Notes and References

1. *In Defense of Ignorance* (New York, 1965), pp. 207-208.

2. Louis D. Rubin, Jr., "The Search for Lost Innocence: Karl Shapiro's *The Bourgeois Poet*," *The Hollins Critic*, I (December, 1964), 8.

3. *Poems, 1940-1953* (New York, 1953), p. 127.

4. *How Does a Poem Mean?* (Boston, 1959), p. 915.

5. *Trial of a Poet* (New York, 1947), pp. 1-22.

6. *Achievement in American Poetry* (Chicago, 1951), p. 102.

7. Rubin, p. 4.

8. Laurence Perrine and James M. Reid, *100 American Poems of the Twentieth Century* (New York, 1966), p. 222.

9. C. F. Main and Peter J. Seng, *Poems* (Belmont, California, 1965), p. 29.

10. Babette Deutsch, *Poetry in Our Time* (Garden City, N.Y., 1963), p. 417.

11. Sam Bradley, "Shapiro Strikes at the Establishment," *University of Kansas City Review*, XXIX (Summer, 1963). 278.

12. See especially pp. 37, 44, 51, 59. For a critique of Shapiro's views on Pound and Eliot, see Alfred Kazin, *Contemporaries* (Boston, 1962), pp. 489-493. Kazin faults Shapiro for taking the "*other* intellectual line of anti-intellectualism."

13. *A Primer for Poets* (Lincoln, Nebraska, 1953), p. 3.

14. See *The Carleton Miscellany*, V (Summer, 1964), 6.

15. "The Contextual Symbol: Karl Shapiro's Image of 'The Jew,' " *American Quarterly*, XVIII (Summer, 1966), 225.

16. Paul Engle and Joseph Langland, eds., *Poet's Choice* (New York, 1962), p. 133. In spite of this, Shapiro's distinction between prose and poetry is worth noting as found in "Prosody and Meaning," *Poetry*, LXXIII (March, 1949), 336-351.

17. "The Innocent," *Nineteen Stories* (New York, 1955), pp. 45-49.

18. "The Witches are Flying," *Oberlin Quarterly*, I (Winter-Spring, 1964), 6.

19. "Karl Shapiro: The Paradox of Prose and Poetry," *Western Review*, XVIII (Spring, 1954), 226.

20. "Author's Comment," *Oberlin Quarterly*, I (Winter-Spring, 1964), 29.

III

Robert Lowell: Protestor as Link Between Past and Present

WE ARE LOOKING for a pattern of development in contemporary protest poetry. We have seen that Eberhart's work contains two of the main themes: war and death. He also writes of the mystery of poetry and touches on the subject of the influence of time (not the ravages of time). Men's actions and their consequences are also important ideas developed by Eberhart. However, Eberhart nowhere strikes the tone of personal urgency. He has little to say about his own personal approach to facing or solving problems. His own death is not a subject over which Eberhart continually broods. Shapiro writes of death and war, also. He expands the latter by including violence of several types (a car crash, for example) and his mention of racial strife is in a subheading under the category of violence. Shapiro's notion of time is that of a corrupting agent. He admittedly moves from early innocence to the loss of this innocence through knowledge. (However, Shapiro's development here is different from Blake's whose idea of "Experience" is differentiated from rather than opposed to "Innocence.") While the mystery of creativity is not a subject in Shapiro's poetry, he does discuss the topic at length in lectures and essays. Thus Eberhart indicates some themes. Shapiro includes these but gives us the additional element of personal literary rebellion. It is a confusing and inconsistent kind of rebellion, but it is a much more individualized response, in tone and in fact, to his poetic subjects than Eberhart is willing to render.

Robert Lowell responds in a personal way to the problems his poetry raises and he responds in a personal way to the social problems of his day as well. His poetry is frequently brooding in tone, particularly when death and war are the subjects. He expands violence to include the violence of personal relationships, of sexuality, of the violence of capitalism. His response to the social ills as he understands them is deeply personal, but essentially negative. He refused to participate in World War II and became a conscientious objector. He has been active in anti-war and civil rights demonstrations more recently and in 1965 refused President Johnson's invitation to a White House arts festival because "every serious artist knows that he cannot enjoy public celebration without making subtle public commitments."[1]

Robert Traill Spence Lowell was born in Boston, Massachusetts, on March 1, 1917. He attended St. Mark's School and then went to Harvard for almost two years. He completed his formal education at Kenyon College in 1940. Among his mentors were John Crowe Ransom, Randall Jarrell, and Richard Eberhart. In 1943 Lowell made two attempts to enlist in the service but was twice rejected. Later, when he was drafted, Lowell refused to serve because he felt the U.S. was no longer endangered and he denounced the indiscriminate bombings of civilians by Allied planes as unprincipled murder. Lowell served five months in a federal prison as a conscientious objector, the same institution, at Danbury, Connecticut, to which Daniel Berrigan would be sent a generation later.

In 1944 his first book of poems was published, *Land of Unlikeness*. Much of what appeared here was included in *Lord Weary's Castle* (1946). For this volume he earned the Pulitzer Prize for poetry. In 1947, still before the age of 30, Lowell won a Guggenheim Fellowship and received a grant of $1000 from the National Institute of Arts and Letters. For two years he was Consultant in Poetry at the Library of Congress. In 1951 he published *The Mills of the Kavanaughs* and eight years later *Life Studies*. For this last he earned the National Book Award (1960). He has lectured on poetry and taught at the State University of Iowa, the Kenyon School of English, Boston University, and the Salzburg Seminar in American Studies in Austria. It is obvious that Lowell had sufficient reason to be interested in the preservation of the "establishment."

The brother of Lowell's great-grandfather was James Russell Lowell and Amy Lowell was a distant cousin of his. These relationships remind us of important background information about Lowell—his roots in New England.

It is Louis Untermeyer who perhaps best sets the tone for our examination of Lowell's work when he says that "Beneath the surface formalism of the verse, there is a deep protest against what New England has become, against the commercialism of the age and the degeneration of the community."[2] Alongside this we might properly acknowledge a comment of Randall Jarrell's in his review of *Lord Weary's Castle*. He says that the poems here "understand the world as a sort of conflict of opposites."[3] Here, then, is what we have: protest, but not a cutting off from the past as revealed by both the content and the "formalism of the verse"; a "conflict of opposites" which results in few, if any, solutions; a tragic tone; and anything but the optimism of the Jungian who posits a union of opposites.

Lowell's greatest protesting is found in what may be obliquely referred to as war poetry. There is little of the gory detail of battle in Lowell's work as is found in the poetry of Eberhart and Shapiro. There is more of the general disgust or shame about war in Lowell's books, however, than is found in the other two writers. Of 1945 he writes, "The world out-Herods Herod . . . ." Lowell tells one interviewer that for this generation, "violence isn't boring."[4] He continues,

We have a thing for the Western movie: some sort of faith that the man who can draw most quickly is the real hero. He's proved himself. Yet that is a terribly artificial standard; the real hero might be someone who'd never get his pistol out of his holster, stumbling about, near-sighted. We don't want to admit that. It's deep in us that the man who draws first somehow has proved himself.

The problem, and the resulting confusion, is in the idealism that "justifies" violence:

I always think there are two great symbolic figures that stand behind American ambition and culture. One is Milton's Lucifer and the other is Captain Ahab: these two sublime ambitions that are doomed and ready, for their idealism, to face any amount of violence . . . .

. . . We might blow up Cuba to save ourselves and then the whole world would blow up. Yet it would come in the guise of an idealistic stroke. (Alvarez, p. 42)

It is not inevitable or uncontrollable war that Lowell speaks against in his writings. For him there is no such thing. Rather, it is the violence that a responsible humanity perpetrates that horrifies Lowell. (It is what Max Brod would call "ignoble suffering," man made, capable of being eliminated. This is unlike, "noble suffering" over which man has no control.[5]) De Sales Standerwick, in concluding an incisive article on Lowell, indicates the poet's stance. He says that for Lowell, into this life "comes greed; greed for land, which is imperialism; greed for money, which is capitalism;[6] greed for power, which is war; greed for sex, which is incest and infidelity; greed for man-made religion, which is Puritanism; greed for one's self, which is suicide."[7] Therefore, as Richard Fein can say in one article, Lowell is preoccupied with the "military leader as butcher,"[8] and in a later article repeat that "The terrible shadow of Napoleon (and Caesar), the leader of absolute destruction, haunts Lowell's poetry . . . ."[9] Proof of these statements is easily

[50]

found in Lowell's *corpus*, including his most current work. In "Christmas Eve Under Hooker's Statue"[10] we read "The cannon of the Common cannot stun / the blundering butcher as he rides on Time—." Another relatively early poem, "Napoleon Crosses the Berezina" (*Castle*, p. 40), begins:

> Here Charlemagne's stunted shadow plays charades
> With pawns and bishops whose play-cannister
> Shivers the Snowman's bones, and the Great Bear
> Shuffles away to his ancestral shades,
> For here Napoleon Bonaparte parades;

The very awfulness of the word "parades" here illustrates Lowell's ideas about the military hierarchy. The rest of the poem follows;

> Hussar and cuirassier and grenadier
> Ascend the tombstone steppes to Russia. Here
> The eagles gather as the West invades
> The Holy Land of Russia. Lord and glory
> Of dragonish, unfathomed waters, rise!
> Although your Berezina cannot gnaw
> These soldier-plumed pontoons to matchwood, ice
> Is turning them to tumbrils, and the snow
> Blazes its carrion-miles to Purgatory.

The value of this poem in relation to Lowell's thoughts on war in much of his work was well expressed by Standerwick (p. 79) who wrote;

All wars are alike; to express continuity, the poet depicts Napoleon as "Charlemagne's stunted shadow." Dreaming dreams, Napoleon marched into Russia, which will contain for him only "tombstone steppes." In 1812, Napoleon was retreating from Moscow; in November of that year, the Russian forces attacked him as he was crossing the Berezina River. Tremendous losses were inflicted upon the would-be conqueror. At that same river, in July, 1941, a fierce battle raged while the

Germans were marching on Smolensk. Again we get the sense of continuity of history. The poet calls upon the God of the "dragonish, unfathomed waters" to come up and wreak havoc on the war-monger. The river cannot chew up the bridges; but it is just as effectively changing them into tumbrils, the wicked, little carts that led the condemned Frenchmen to the guillotine during the Revolution. Add to the river the paralyzing snow and Napoleon's journey becomes truly "carrion-miles to Purgatory."

When war becomes a favorite pastime of leaders and nations, then really "we are poured out like water," we are wasted, we are condemned. It only remains for the eagles to hover over the place where the bodies shall be. Nor does Robert Lowell assuage the harsh tenor of his words, for war has stalked its prey too long and too doggedly.

The words "we are poured out like water" are from another early poem, "The Quaker Graveyard in Nantucket" (*Castle*, p. 141). Austin Warren calls it an "admirable elegy" and Hugh Staples in his book on Lowell calls the work "a major poem of sustained brilliance, which challenges comparison with the great elegies of the language."[11] Richard Fein joins the praise when he cites this as "the most moving elegy written during the war ... ("War Poetry," p. 826). Fein sees the kind of conflict Jarrell noted earlier operating here: "It is the contradiction between the harsh and repeated reality of man's death at sea and the envisioned promise of his dominion over nature that the poem must resolve." He notes that the poem united one sailor's death, at war, with the deaths of a great number of sailors destroyed in that same war, and then many more previous deaths at sea. "Atlantic, you are fouled with the blue sailors." (Earlier in this poem Lowell writes that "only bones abide/ There in the nowhere . . . ." This gives the piece a kind of meditative value and symbol recalling Eberhart's "The Groundhog.") The attempted resolution is in a Judgment Day and whether or not this works in the poem each reader will have to determine.

Untermeyer says of Lowell that there is "no escaping the moral purpose of his work" (p. 662), and on that we must insist. A brief discussion of "The Dead in Europe" is appropriate here. It is a prayer to Mary by those killed in the war. These dead seek to be reborn in paradise, to be rescued from their state of death. The first two stanzas end with the same line, "Our sacred Earth in our day was our curse." The third and last stanza ends with a tense variation, changing "was" to "is." Pathetic as the appeal is, it is more than just an appeal for rebirth. As one critic noticed, "The poem is an expression of the need for a spiritual recovery after war" (Fein, "War Poetry," p. 832). This places the work directly beside Eberhart's "Aesthetics after War" as a plea for sanity.

While this may appear to be a poem that might be considered in an optimistic vein, the thrust of Lowell's message seems anything but that. This is true even of what might be called his Catholic poetry. (Lowell converted to the Roman Catholic Church and left it several years later.) John Bayley (p. 85) notes that "In an age when destruction and madness oppress the poet, like every other citizen, Lowell has learnt not to write about these things but to take them on . . . " Eight pages earlier Bayley had said that "Lowell's poetry looks out in an unexpected direction. It yearns towards non-existence. If a poetry can be said to have the death-wish, it has it." R. K. Meiners has noted that in the poetry of Lowell, as in Tate's, "the person, isolated in the moment, feels the narrow dimensions of his mortality pressing on him . . ." while Philip Cooper also discusses the death wish in Lowell poetry.[14]

Death as a result of war can be an obvious theme for a poet. The more depressing aspects of death itself, however, haunt Lowell. He has composed poems like "Her Dead Brother" (*Castle*, p. 104), "In Memory of Arthur Winslow" (*Castle*, p. 25), "Mary Winslow" (*Castle*, p. 31), and a host more including many free adaptations that appear in *Imitations*. These include all five of the selections by Francois

Villon[15], Giacomo Leopardi's "Sylvia" (p. 29), Johann Peter Hebel's "Sic Transit" (p. 32), Heinrich Heine's "Heine, Dying in Paris" (p. 38), Victor Hugo's "At Gautier's Grave" (p. 34), and a number of others.

Peter Viereck talks of the great "sense of the tragic" (see Untermeyer, p. 662) in Lowell's work. This is found not only in face and in subject matter but in individual lines as well. In "Colloquy in Black Rock" (*Castle*, p. 11) we find, "All Discussions/ End in the mud-flat detritus of death." In the long poem, "The Mills of the Kavanaughs" (*Castle*, pp. 81-100) we read the rhetorical question with response, "Is it throwing money down/ A well to help the poor? They die." In "The Banker's Daughter"[16] we find these lines:

> Now seasons cycle to the laughing ring
> of scything children; king must follow king
> and walk the plank to his immortal leap.

In a two-part poem, "David and Bathsheba in the Public Garden" (*Castle*, p. 10) the first section ends with the words, "Surely, I will not die." The closing words of the second segment are the opposite, "I must surely die."

In some poems death is seen in relation to time, especially in *Imitations* as in "The Voyage" (Baudelaire, p. 66). "Between the Porch and the Altar" (*Castle*, p. 47) has hints of the relationship of death and life and there is even an address to Arthur Winslow who seemed to feel that somehow money could conquer death:

> ... for what else could bring
> You, Arthur, to the veined and alien West
> But the devil's notions that your gold at least
> Could give back life to men who whipped or backed
> the King. (*Castle*, p. 25)

It must be pointed out that Lowell's pessimism goes beyond the subject of death. It penetrates his religious thinking. There are some bright moments, of course.

"Where the Rainbow Ends" (*Castle*, p. 75) concludes with "Stand and live,/ The dove has brought an olive branch to eat." There is also in "Jonathan Edwards in Western Massachusetts" the perhaps comforting idea that "hope lives in doubt./ Faith is trying to do without/ faith." Such examples hardly balance the rest, however. There is the fear that "God/ Abandoned us to Satan ..." in "After the Surprising Conversions" (*Castle*, p. 66). There is also the very convincing poem "Mr. Edwards and the Spider" (*Castle*, p. 64).[17] Here is what Laurence Perrine says about this poem (which asks Edwards' question, "What are we in the hands of the great God?"):

> The real subject of Edwards' discourse is death and damnation. In stanzas one and four, spiders are pictured as the victims of death; in stanza three, as an agent of death; in stanza five (the Black Widow) as a metaphor for death. Death is inevitable for all men, Edwards argues, and for all but a few it is followed by a damnation of inconceivable torment and of infinite duration. Edwards' Calvinistic theology—his belief in original sin, in predestination, in the littleness of man, and in the absolute sovereignty of God—is clearly seen in this poem. In the first stanza the light lives and deaths of spiders suggest symbolically the inevitable destiny and destruction of men. Stanza two points out the powerlessness of man to combat his inherent sinfulness—which foredooms him to damnation—by any effort of the will. He plays against "a sickness" past his cure—"the fire/ And treason crackling" in his blood. Stanza three reemphasizes the powerlessness of man to prevent death. Stanza four describes the casting of the sinful soul into the eternal fire, from which no struggle or strength can save it. Stanza five, addressed particularly to Josiah Hawley, describes the torment and the duration of eternal punishment. To be punished, thus is "To die and know it"—to die yet not lose consciousness—to die and yet suffer, indescribably, forever.[18]

Care must be taken not to misread the poem, not arbitrarily to substitute Lowell's voice for Edwards', to mistake the narrator of a poem for the poet. However, this is not the only poem of its kind in Lowell's work, nor are the sentiments expressed here unique in Lowell's work. "Never to have lived is best" (*Castle*, p. 48); that was written by Robert Lowell. In *Imitations* he renders two lines from Heine thus: "sleep is lovely, death is better still,/ not to have been born is of course the miracle." Another Lowell poem ends,

> It is all
> A moment. The trees
> Grow earthward: neither good
> Nor evil, hopes nor fears,
> Repulsion nor desire,
> Earth, water, air or fire
> Will serve to stay the fall.

(*Castle*, p. 36)

Hayden Carruth comes closest to understanding Lowell's pessimism: it is the

expression of the radical guilt which seems to be at the base of Lowell's poetic nature. It is a guilt which took form like any other, leaving aside psychoanalytical factors: first from elements of generalized cultural guilt, in Lowell's case the New Englander's shame over the Indians and the Salem women, which has exercised an obviously powerful influence on his imagination; then from the guilt that all men feel, with deep necessity, for the deaths of their own fathers; and finally from the horrendous events of contemporary history. But what is the punishment for the crimes that produce this pervading guilt? It is personal death. We all know this, from the first moment of our mortal recognition. Yet against this Lowell casts again and again his instinctive belief in the remission of sin, or rather his knowledge, his feeling, of his own undiminished innocence. Then what can our death be? What is our guilt? There is only one answer, outside of absurdity. Our death is our sin, for which we pay in advance through our guilt. Our death is a crime against every good principle in the universe: nature, God, the human heart. Yet we, the innocent, are the responsible one—this is the idea Lowell cannot forego. We carry this crime, like a seed, within us. Our bodies are going to commit it, do what we will. They are going to carry out this murder, inexorably, while we stand by, helpless and aghast.[19]

Thus in spite of an undoubted Catholic influence on Lowell's work ("I think becoming a Catholic convert had a good deal to do with writing again"), Peter Viereck is no doubt correct in saying it would be an error to place Lowell in the tradition of Catholic poets.[20] Lowell's own remarks support this to a degree at least. In an interview he said ". . . I won't say the Catholicism gave me subject matter, but it gave me some kind of form . . . ." Hayden Carruth goes even further, saying that most of Lowell's good work is not religious in the strict sense of the term at all. The better works, even those apparently religious, like "Mr. Edwards and the Spider" and "After the Surprising Conversions" (*Castle*, pp. 66-67), find that "a large part of their meaning is a stable and predictable element of the general cultural situation, with which the poems are, so to speak, invested" (Carruth, p. 438).

Lowell finds it important to connect himself with the past. Perhaps for a New Englander, apparently hounded by the past as Nathaniel Hawthorne seemed to be, this is an absolute necessity. He could be no American Adam as R. W. B. Lewis presents this new man.[21] He has his roots and perhaps his guilt is a necessary consequence. It has certainly given Lowell a respect for not only the content, but the form of the past. Christopher Ricks compares Lowell to Ben Jonson and notes that "both create a poetry which is profoundly classical in its memory of dignity and yet profoundly of its own time in its sense of turbulence."[22] Lowell remembers Ford Madox Ford's early advice to him: "Ford was rather flippant about it, said of course you've got to learn classics, you'll just cut yourself off from humanity if you don't. I think that's always given me some sort of yardstick for English." Lowell makes similar remarks in another interview in 1963.[23]

This ongoing discussion of Lowell's is related to his work in *Life Studies*. He has fifteen confessional poems[24] in Part Four of this book and in these poems he examines the idea that experience and art melt together and influence each other. In "Home after Three Months Away" for example, Lowell sees his current problems as a consequence of the particular past he has inherited. The past, for Lowell, bears on man's art, it bears on his life. This is particularly evident in his poems on other writers like Hart Crane (*Life Studies*, p. 55) and George Santayana.[25] Thus Lowell has been able to observe, "It is harder to be a good man than a good poet."[26] Jay Martin concludes from his analysis of Lowell's work that "his basic subject has always been the fate of selfhood in time, and his basic method the examination of the convergence in man of past history and present circumstance" (p. 7).

No doubt it is true that Lowell, of the poets we are considering, is most immersed in Western tradition. This may, to some at least, give more effectiveness to his protesting. It is probably the reason why, of all the poets we are discussing, his poetry is the most melodic. We can close this portion of our investigation by simply quoting the first poem from *Lord Weary's Castle*, Lowell's first book (excluding limited editions). This early poem has more music in it than any of our other protest poets could compose in one poem—and than some in their entire body of works. Here is "The Exile's Return":

> There mounts in squalls a sort of rusty mire,
> Not ice, not snow, to leaguer the Hotel De
> Ville, where braced pig-iron dragons grip
> The blizzard to their rigor mortis. A bell
> Grumbles when the reverberations strip,
> The thatching from its spire,

Robert Lowell

The search-guns click and spit and split up timber
And nick the slate roofs on the Holstenwall
Where torn-up tilestones crown the victor. Fall
And winter, spring and summer, guns unlimber
And lumber down the narrow gabled street
Past your gray, sorry and ancestral house
Where the dynamited walnut tree
Shadows a squat, old, wind-torn gate and cows
The Yankee commandant. You will not see
Strutting children or meet
The peg-leg and reproachful chancellor
With a forget-me-not in his button-hole
When the unseasoned liberators roll
Into the Market Square, ground arms before
The Rathaus; but already lily-stands
Burgeon the risen Rhineland, and a rough
Cathedral lifts its eye. Pleasant enough,
Voi ch' entrate, and your life is in your hands.

(Castle, p. 9)

Notes and References

1. Jay Martin, *Robert Lowell* (Minneapolis, 1970), p. 41.

2. *Modern American Poetry* (New York, 1962), p. 662.

3. Quoted in *The American Tradition in Literature*, edited by Sculley Bradley, Richmond Croom Beatty and E. Hudson Long (New York, 1967 [Volume 2], p. 1646.

4. A. Alvarez, "A Talk with Robert Lowell," *Encounter*, XXIV (February, 1965), 42.

5. See *Paganism—Christianity—Judaism* (University, Alabama, 1970).

6. See Randall Jarrell, "The Kingdom of Necessity," in *Robert Lowell*, edited by Michael London and Robert Boyers (New York, 1970), p. 21. Jarrell says, "Mr. Lowell has Weber's unconvincing belief in the necessary connection between capitalism and Calvinism."

7. DeSales Standerwick, "Notes on Robert Lowell," *Renascence*, VIII (Winter, 1955), 83.

8. Richard Fein, "The Trying-Out of Robert Lowell," *Sewanee Review*, LXXII (Winter, 1964), 133.

9. Richard Fein, "Mary and Bellona: The War Poetry of Robert Lowell," *Southern Review*, I (Autumn, 1965), 823.

10. Robert Lowell, *Lord Weary's Castle and The Mills of the Kavanaughs* (New York, 1961), p. 23.

11. Quoted in John Bayley's "Robert Lowell: The Poetry of Cancellation," *London Magazine*, VI (June, 1966), 76.

12. In a more recent group of poems, printed in *The New York Review of Books* (April 24, 1969), pp. 8-9, Lowell returns to the theme of the military leader. The titles of some of the poems are

illustrative: "Atilla," "The Death of Count Roland," "Tamerlane Old," "The Army of the Duc de Nemours," and "Old Hickory."

13. Bayley, p. 77.

14. R. K. Meiners, *Everything to Be Endured* (Columbia, Missouri, 1970), p. 33; Philip Cooper, *The Autobiographical Myth of Robert Lowell* (Chapel Hill, North Carolina, 1970). See especially p. 86.

15. *Imitations* (New York, 1961), pp. 8-24.

16. Robert Lowell, *Life Studies* (New York, 1959), p. 5.

17. See Bradley's discussion of this poem, p. 1647.

18. Laurence Perrine and James M. Reid, *100 American Poems of the Twentieth Century* (New York, 1966), p. 244.

19. "A Meaning of Robert Lowell," *Hudson Review*, XX (Autumn, 1967), 439.

20. See Richard James Calhoun, "The Poetic Metamorphosis of Robert Lowell," *Furman Studies*, XI (November, 1963), 11. Allen Tate agrees that "Lowell is consciously a Catholic poet" (London and Boyers, p. 1). For a dissenting opinion see Marius Bewley's chapter in *Robert Lowell*, edited by Michael London and Robert Boyers (New York, 1970), p. 6.

21. See R. W. B. Lewis, *The American Adam* (Chicago, 1965).

22. Christopher Ricks, "The Three Lives of Robert Lowell," *New Statesman* (March 26, 1965), p. 496.

23. See "Robert Lowell in Conversation with A. Alvarez," *Review*, No. 8 (August, 1963), p. 38.

24. See Lowell, *Life Studies*, pp. 59-90.

25. *Ibid.*, p. 51. An exception to this insistence on the influence of the poet as a writer is Lowell's poem "For Theodore Roethke," in *Near the Ocean* (New York, 1967), pp. 51-52.

26. Quoted in Martin, p. 43.

IV

Allen Ginsberg: The Shock of Despair

IT IS BECOMING more apparent, even to the lay reader, that there is no subject matter unfit for poetry. Among so many others, Allen Ginsberg would say that if something is a part of life it may be a subject for poetry. William Carlos Williams wrote of certain contemporary poetry in his Introduction to Ginsberg's early poems, *Empty Mirror* (San Francisco, 1961):

> A new sort of line, omitting memories of trees and water-courses and clouds and pleasant glades—exists today. It is measured by the passage of time without accent, monotonous, useless—unless you are drawn as Dante was to see the truth, undressed, and to sway to a beat that is far removed from the beat of dancing feet but rather finds in the shuffling of human beings in all the stages of their day, the trip to the bathroom, to the stairs of the subway, the steps of the office or factory routine the mystical measure of their passions.

What Williams calls "the truth, undressed" is indeed what Allen Ginsberg is consciously trying to render. He says so himself in a poem praising another writer, "On Burroughs' Work":

> The method must be purest meat
>   and no symbolic dressing,
> actual visions & actual prisons
>   as seen then and now.[1]

After a stanza, Ginsberg refers to a specific work of Burroughs and includes a phrase, while embellishing a metaphor, which gives the title to one of his own collections of poems:

> A naked lunch is natural to us,
>   we eat reality sandwiches.
> But allegories are so much lettuce.
> Don't hide the madness.

It is, perhaps, in revealing the madness that Ginsberg has drawn so much attention. Not only is he revealing it, but he is doing so "madly." (The poet's father, Louis Ginsberg, himself a poet, criticizes Allen's work for being too much a surrealistic outpouring of the subconscious. "He goes to extremes."[2])

One of the "extremes" that obviously irritates people is Ginsberg's use of language; language that some consider obscene, that some consider blasphemous, that some consider unpatriotic has disturbed many readers. (The terms "obscene," "blasphemous" and "unpatriotic" may seem inappropriately lumped together here, yet a point to be made is that much of Ginsberg's "obscenity" is aimed at nationalism, that false patriotism, and at self-delusion, that false religion.)

Obscene words are a part of today's literature and specifically a part of Allen Ginsberg's work because they form an integral part of what the poet is trying to do. Indeed, as I shall try to indicate in the discussion of "Wichita Vortex Sutra," in Marshall McLuhan's terms, the medium is the message. However, it may not be inappropriate to touch, briefly, on the use, in general, of obscenities in literature. In "Obscene Words and the Function of Literature,"[3] Lawrence W. Hyman observes that "there is agreement among critics that the immediate and prime function of literature is to make us see and feel the object or human situation in a way that we have never done before." Two

paragraphs later Hyman writes; "We are supposed to be
startled by the obscenity; but only in the same way as we
are startled by an unusual comparison, or by a catachresis
or an oxymoron." Hyman also says that "the shock we feel
on seeing the work is the shock we're supposed to feel at
what has happened . . . ." Too many readers, however, fail
to make the switch from the word to the situation. They
are startled by the obscenity itself, not the condition it
represents. This discussion of language should be carried a
step further. Language, particularly as it is developed in
literature, in formulaic conversation, in advertising, for
example, becomes dangerously ambiguous. It is liable to
various interpretations. One has only to witness the understanding and misunderstanding of recent papal pronounce-
ments to prove the point. In an article subtitled "Corrupting the word," Joseph Blenkinsopp wrote this:

> Political (in the pejorative sense of ideological) language is
> language subjugated to the pursuit of power and influence.
> What marks it out in the first place is its non-reciprocating
> character, a use of key symbols and cliches as focal points of
> sentiment and a studied ambiguity of expression especially
> when an outright statement might prove embarrassing . . . .
> Much of the fascination exercised by Senator [Eugene] Mc-
> Carthy on the public during his campaign must be explained by
> his disavowal of political jargon and rhetoric in favor of a
> direct, clear, almost matter-of-fact way of speaking.[4]

The basis for Blenkinsopp's article was a blast by the
former priest Charles Davis at the Catholic Church for its
"corruption of the word," a phrase borrowed from Robert
Adolfs who himself took it from the philosopher Joseph
Pieper.

Ambiguity is precisely what Ginsberg and others who use
obscenities in their work are rebelling against. We shall see
how Ginsberg puts this idea to work in a particular poem,
but for the moment, suffice it to say that from one point
of view, corruption of the word, ambiguity of the word,

results in a tragedy of confusion. We have heard many political figures say many ambiguous words about certain situations or other political figures, and could not be sure of the meaning of their words. However, when Eldridge Cleaver said "Fuck [Governor Ronald] Reagan,"[5] we all understood his message. Perhaps we could say that he startled us and therefore got his feelings across. With this in mind then, let us turn to the poetic work of Allen Ginsberg.

While Ginsberg cannot be identified as a prolific poet, he has published consistently. Even so, if most readers of contemporary poetry were asked to name some of his poems by title, the number mentioned would probably be limited to half dozen or so, including "Howl," "Kaddish," "Wichita Vortex Sutra," "A Supermarket in California," "Sunflower Sutra," and one or two others. Ginsberg has not written many memorable lines. His verse is not the kind that is frequently committed to memory. He creates moods that admirers may attempt to re-create in recalling his work. He also creates an outstanding image, but his attempts at rendering powerful images are rare. What we are left with, then, is either a sense of the integrity of the poet or a kind of horror at his audacity, his presumptuousness, perhaps even a horror due to his honesty concerning his own personal life.

Ginsberg uses the poet's materials, words, in his unique way. It is, in a sense, his vocabulary that has disgusted and thrilled readers. Legally, his famous poem "Howl" was judged not to be obscene. This poem has been described as "the extreme protest of the Beat Generation."[6] Yet Judge Clayton W. Horn was sympathetic to what Ginsberg was attempting to accomplish in terms which must have gratified the author and which described rather precisely Ginsberg's approach:

Life is not encased in one formula whereby everyone acts the same or conforms to a particular pattern. No two persons think alike. We are all made from the same mould, but in different patterns. Would there be any freedom of press or speech if one must reduce his vocabulary to vapid innocuous euphemism? An author should be real in treating his subject and be allowed to express his thoughts and ideas in his own words.

While someone of the stature of Flannery O'Connor would criticize the writers of the Beat Generation for their lack of restraint, I think that Ginsberg would say that this criticism should rather be directed at advertisers and war makers than at himself. Immodest language ought not to be confused with unrestrained use of vocabulary. The poem that proves this point is "Wichita Vortex Sutra," which, along with "Howl," may be preparatory poems for an attempted epic poem by Ginsberg.

"Wichita Vortex Sutra" is a poem written in opposition to the U.S. involvement in Vietnam. In it the poet attempts to make a mantra of the American language. In doing this, he declares an end to the war even as it continues. Ginsberg defines a mantra as a "short magic formula usually involving an aspect of the Divine, usually given as meditation exercise by guru to student, sometimes sung in community or 'kirtan'—the formula is considered to be identical with the god named, and have inevitable power attached to its pronunciation. Oft used in chanting or invocation."[7] The brilliant way Ginsberg uses this "device" in "Wichita Vortex Sutra"[8] is what gives the poem its distinctive and distinguished features.

That language itself may deserve the attention Ginsberg gives it is indicated in the poem itself:

> The war is language,
>   language abused
>   for Advertisement,
>   language used
> like magic for power on the planet: (ll. 282-286)

Ginsberg once said in a conversation: "All public reality's a script, and anybody can write the script the way he wants. The warfare's psychic now. Whoever controls the language, the images, controls the race. Power all boils down to whether McNamara gets up on the right side of the bed. And who's McNamara anyway? He's a lot of TV dots. That's public reality. Like imagine what would happen if McNamara got on television and started saying, 'Some of the fellows, some of the human beings we've been fighting with' instead of 'some of the Communists.' Words like 'Communist,' 'capitalist'—they're language as hypnosis, as an outrage against feeling. They're not the reality we know in the bedroom; they're comic strip reality. They ought to be printed in the papers in those little balloons."[9] Paul Carroll has written that "When language is twisted and deprived of its primary function—that is, to describe the truth of men and events—then a nation may well be on the road toward barbarism, immoral aggression and slaughter for the sake of slaughter" (pp. 108-109). Carroll says this in a valuable discussion of "Wichita Vortex Sutra" which has influenced much of what follows in this analysis.

Given a poem like "Wichita" it is difficult to say whether the poet's life style flows from his poetry or vice-versa. It seems a chicken-egg question, and a real one. Pulitzer Prize winning poet Louis Simpson has written that "Hemingway created the life-style of the Lost Generation; Ginsberg created that of the Beat. If was a spectacular achievement."[10] Like "Howl," its predecessor in a special way that some of Ginsberg's earlier poems are not, "Wichita" is in three parts. Since it is a poem about language as much as it is about war and race problems, language is the key to the three divisions. The protest in this poem is primarily one against the abuse of language.[11] The first and largest section of "Wichita" covers 511 of 689 lines. It contains a virtuoso display, a *tour de force*, of language abused. The second section is the making of the mantra, beginning with line 512 and probably ending at 561, although there is ambiguity here. The final 127 lines contain a recognition by the poet of the failure of his mantra.

The first 511 lines contain as much frankness and resentment as the poem seems able to bear. We read of "the Methodist minister with cracked eyes/ leaning over the table/ quoting Kierkegaard 'death of God'/ a million dollars/ in the bank   owns all West Wichita/ came to Nothing!" (ll. 34-39). The full damning effect of this passage can be understood if related to other Ginsberg utterances about money. In "Sunflower Sutra"[12] he contemptuously writes of "rubber dollar bills" while in "Howl" we read of "Moloch whose blood is running money!"[13] In another poem Ginsberg asks of money, "Is this the God of Gods ...?"[14] and his reply is implicit in his question. In still another work he laments of "money and arguments of great affairs,/ the culture of my generation ...."[15] "Death of Van Gogh's Ear" begins;

> Poet is Priest
> Money has reckoned the soul of America
> Congress broken thru to the precipice of Eternity
> The President built a War machine which will
>   vomit and rear up Russia out of Kansas[16]

and the same poem ends four pages later:

> Money! Money! Money! shrieking mad celestial money of
>   illusion! Money made of nothing, starvation, suicide!
>   Money of failure! Money of death!
> Money against Eternity! and eternity's strong mills
>   grind out vast paper of Illusion!

While it is characteristic of Ginsberg to see money in terms of the evil it can support, especially "a War machine," his most blatant poem about money was written in 1958 titled "American Change" (*Sandwiches*, pp. 67-69). In this work he examines various pieces of U.S. currency and reflects on their significance, what they mean to men, what they will buy. A $5.00 bill, for example, can be put to work at a racetrack, provide a hotel room, purchase heroin or be a generous present to the blind. The poem is very much like Michael Quoist's "Prayer Before a Twenty-Dollar Bill"[17] wherein the poet reflects how money "can serve or destroy man." Individual lines from the poem, all reflecting on the $20, will give an idea of its content:

> It will never reveal all the struggles and efforts
>   it represents, all the disillusionment and
>   slighted dignity ...
> It has offered white roses to the radiant fiance ...
> It has paid for the saving visit of the doctor ...
> It has paid for the death of the baby in its
>   mother's womb ...
> It has produced the movie unfit for children ...
> It has bought for a few hours the body of a woman.

Untitled poems by Robert Marshall Haven in *Look at Us, Lord* are also on a similar theme.[18]

Ginsberg, of course, does not stop with money. Its worship is merely a symbol for him. It is a false image, a minted idol. He can easily move from the item, money, to the men who are the power behind the money:

> How big is the prick of the President?
>   How big is Cardinal Viet-Nam?
> How little the prince of the F.B.I., unmarried all
>   these years!
> the prince
> How big are all the Public Figures?
> What kind of flesh hangs, hidden behind their Images?

> (*Planet*, p. 112).

Their images, just like the image a nation officially tries to project of itself, are built of language. It is, however, language abused, as this passage indicates:

[70]

> Not Hanoi our enemy
> Not China our enemy
> The Viet Cong!
> MacNamara [sic] made a "bad guess"
> "Bad Guess" chorused the Reporters?
> Yes, no more than a Bad Guess, in 1962
> > "8000 American Troops handle the
> > Situation" (ll. 167-174)

There is more about American guessing and then this on the relationship between prosperity and war:

> American Eagle beating its wings over Asia
> million dollar helicopters
> a billion dollars worth of Marines (ll. 201-203)

This is followed again by headlines of ambiguity:

> Omaha World Herald — *Rusk Says Toughness*
> > *Essential for Peace*

and

> Lincoln Nebraska Morning Star —
> > *Vietnam War Brings Prosperity*

However the poet sees these only as

> the latest quotation on the human meat market —
> > Father I cannot tell a lie! (ll. 230-231)

A little later comes the insistence that "The war is language,/ language abused/ for Advertisement,/ language used/ like magic for power on the planet . . ." (ll. 282-286).

Ginsberg speaks of the Vietnam war in a language far clearer than that of official Washington:

Are these the towns where the language emerged
   from the mouths here
     that makes a Hell of riots in Dominica
sustains the aging tyranny of Chiang in silent
   Taipeh city
Paid for the lost French war in Algeria
   overthrew the Guatemalan polis in '54
maintaining United Fruit's banana greed
     another thirteen years
for the secret prestige of the Dulles family
   lawfirm? (ll. 376-384)

The passage about the job at United Fruit echoes an earlier poem in the same book where we read of mad billionaires "who own United Fruits and Standard Oil and Hearst The Press/ and Texas NBC and someone owns the Radios owns vast/ Spheres of Air—Subliminal Billionaire got/ State Legislatures filled with Capital Punishment Fiends because/ nobody's been in love on US soil long enough to realize/ We who pay the Public Hangman make State Murder . . ." (p. 22).

What is implied in Ginsberg's attitude concerning war is explicit in the theme of personal responsibility running through his work. In "Wichita Vortex Sutra" the reference to United Fruit is meant to remind us about personal responsibility. In "The Change" the poet refers to his own guilt when he writes "Oh Negro beaten in the eye in my/ home . . ." (*Planet*, p. 58). In another collection Ginsberg appeals: ". . .millions of tons of human wheat were burned in secret/ caverns under the White House/ while India starved and screamed and ate mad dogs . . ." (*Kaddish*, p. 61). The thought is repeated in a more recent poem, "Kral Majales": "and the Capitalists drink gin and whiskey on airplanes but let/ Indian brown millions starve . . ." (*Planet*, p. 89). Ginsberg's response to the world situation is a personal one: ". . . trust your own *personal* reality, trust your visionary responses . . ." (Kramer, p. 90). Thus when Gins-

berg says in "Wichita" that "I here declare the end of the
War!" (l. 545) he knows this does not bring peace in Vietnam but he can confidently and importantly say ' I end the
war in me and anyone who's affected by my gesture
. . . ."[19] This is certainly in the manner of Thoreau who
wrote of his own opposition to a war: "It is true, I might
have resisted forcibly [detention] with more or less effect,
might have run 'amok' against society; but I preferred that
society should run 'amok' against me, it being the desperate
party."[20]

So Ginsberg's appeal in "Wichita" is for personal responsibility in the face of perverted language as used by Secretary McNamara, General Maxwell Taylor, *Life* magazine,
the newspaper, Secretary Dulles, TV, Senator Stennis, and
others. How he reacts is the poem. He shows us the false
language, then makes a mantra of the American language in
the hope that magic will be worked. While riding in his car
he says, beginning in the second division of the poem,

> I call all Powers of imagination
>   to my side in this auto to make Prophecy (ll. 512-513)

and in fifty lines renders the creation of the mantra. What
the mantra itself stands for is a kind of universality of
thought, making one individual's idea of cosmological significance. It has hints of Teilhard's Noosphere, Jung's
Collective Unconscious, Christianity's Mystical Body. It is
as if he were aware that the world will indeed by saved for
the sake of a single just man and that each of us must try
to be that man. However, the poet cannot ask us to be just
men unless he himself makes the attempt—and that is the
meaning of personal responsibility. At the risk of sounding
utopian, he says himself that "Somebody's got to make a
break & contact/ Khruschev [sic] in the Noosphere——"
(*Planet*, p. 12). In another poem he has the realization of
"everybody waiting for one mind/ to break thru—" (*Planet*,
p. 27).

Allen Katzman rightly refers to Ginsberg's "oriental belief in universality"[21] which only echoes the poet's own view of his Blakean self, of seeing "eternity in a flower . . . heaven in a grain of sand."[22] So the making of a mantra is appropriate. What follows, the final section indicating the failure of the mantra, is more puzzling.

In this last part of "Wichita" the mantra maker declares that "The War is gone" (l. 575) but immediately follows with statistics about increased casualties in Vietnam. The following passage shows that Ginsberg continues to equate the war with false words:

> after the Marines killed 256 Vietcong captured 31
> ten day operation Harvest Moon Last December
>   Language language
> U.S. Military Spokesmen
>   Language language
>   Cong death toll
>   has soared to 100 in First Air Cavalry
>   division's Sector of
>   Language language
>   Operation White Wing near Bong Son
> Some of the
>   Language language
>   Communist
>   Language language soldiers
>   charged so desperately
>   they were struck with six or seven bullets
>   before they fell
>   Language language . . . (ll. 590-606)

Then, as if he had just remembered his mantra, the poet says, "The war was over several hours ago!" (l. 609). Thus he can turn to the domestic scene and head "straight to the heart of Wichita!" (l. 625). However, it is more language that he has to hear on the car radio

> *you certainly smell good*
>   the radio says (ll. 630-631)

as he passes "McConnel Airforce Base/ nourishing the city——/" (ll. 645-646). He also passes several business establishments including the Hotel Eaton where, the poet says, Carrie Nation began the Vietnam war with "an angry axe/ attacking Wine—" (ll. 470-471). Now we can see how the poem gets its title:

> Here fifty years ago, by her violence
> began a vortex of hatred that defoliated the Mekong Delta—
> Proud Wichita! vain Wichita
> cast the first stone!— (ll. 471-474)

He even blames this "first stone" with the murdering of his mother whose insanity he alludes to. We are told of the murder in one of Ginsberg's best known works, dedicated to his mother Naomi, the thirty-page "Kaddish" (*Kaddish*, pp. 7-36).

"Wichita's" final five lines indicate the last attempt at success through an unconvincing proclamation of the end of hostilities and again a turning to internal problems:

> The war is over now—
> Except for the souls
> held prisoner in Niggertown
> still pining for love of your tender white bodies O
> children of Wichita!

It is all false bravado, however, and the poet knows it and he expects us to know he knows it. That is the point of the whole poem: heroic failure. The tremendous despair of the poem relates it to so much of what Ginsberg has written before. Very likely a strong case could be made for seeing "Kaddish," "Howl," and "Wichita Vortex Sutra" as a trilogy about the insanity of this technological age as symbolized by the world's most technologically advanced nation. "Kaddish" begins with a single mind destroyed and is very family oriented. "Howl" broadens the perspective to many destroyed minds and is oriented toward a whole generation and its values. The despair grows. In "Wichita" an even greater despair is evident. "Wichita" associates the values of a society to a specific event, the Vietnam War. The unity of tone that sustains these three poems as a trilogy is provided by despair, a tone that is developed in later Ginsberg poetry, as well. "Howl" begins with the well-known line "I saw the best minds of my generation destroyed by madness," and so it is for Ginsberg. William Carlos Williams explains "It is a howl of defeat." But Williams follows these words with an optimism that later Ginsberg work does not bear out: "Not defeat at all, for he has gone through defeat as if it were an ordinary experience, a trivial experience. Everyone in this life is defeated, but a man, if he be a man, is not defeated."[23] Williams has failed to recognize what is implicitly in every Ginsberg poem and what was signaled to us in the first two poems in Ginsberg's earliest published volume of poetry *Empty Mirror* to which Williams himself wrote an "Introduction." The first, untitled poem of the book, ends;

> . . . but now
> I have no hope and I am tired. (p. 7)

On the very next page we read;

> . . .What a
> terrible future. I am twenty-three,
> year of the non birthday,
> gate of darkness.

Ginsberg has gone through the gate but never turned around to walk or even look back. In "After Dead Souls," a poem in the same book (p. 7), the poet sees America rushing to destruction. A few pages later in "Paterson" he writes of a crucified America, resurrected, to be sure, but resurrected to a frenzy "screaming and dancing against the

orchestra in the destructible ballroom/ of the world ..."
(p. 39).

What seems to have affected Ginsberg most is the failure
of democracy, the political ideal. It is evident in much of
his work, perhaps implicit in all. Something, in the guise of
democracy, is interested only in power. In early 1961, in a
poem significantly titled "Who Will Take Over the Universe?" (*Planet*, pp. 7-8), Ginsberg rhetorically asks, "How
many families control the States?" Then he points to an
important truth that he recognizes: "Ignore the Government,/ send your protest to Clint Murchison." Perhaps that
is what Ginsberg is attempting to do via his poetry, to
bypass the government and send his messages directly to
the power holders. If this is so, another cause for the poet's
despair is evidenced, since the people who read Ginsberg
are not the Murchisons. What he really wants is someone to

> Screech out over the radio that Standard Oil
>   is a bunch of
> spying Businessmen intent on building one
>   Standard Oil in
> the whole universe like an egotistical cancer
> and yell on television to England to watch out
>   for United Fruits
> they got Central America by the balls
> nobody but them can talk San Salvador, they
>   run big
> Guatemala puppet armies, gas Dictators, they're
> the Crown of Thorns
> upon the Consciousness of poor Christ-Indian
> Central America, and the Pharisees are US
>
> (*Planet*, p. 19).

Ginsberg's only hope, in fact, seems to rest in poetry
itself. He does indeed wish to be Shelley's unacknowledged
legislator of the world. Hence his use of scriptural language

[77]

and metaphors and liturgical forms is not inappropriate. It is to the highest kind of morality that he is appealing. As Bruce Hunsberger has written, the true Beat Generation is a religious phenomenon and beat really signifies beatitude.[24] While all will not agree with this assessment it must not be overlooked. It is the way that many of the beats see themselves.

For example, Ginsberg, in explaining "Howl," gave the following topic headings to the three part work: "Part 1, a lament for the Lamb in America with instances of remarkable lamblike youths; Part II names the monster of mental consciousness that preys on the Lamb; Part III a litany of affirmation of the Lamb in its glory . . . ."[25] (I might point out that Part III, the "affirmation," is the weakest of the poem's sections. Ginsberg is the better poet as the despairing Ginsberg.)

To go to Ginsberg himself, again, the pessimistic citizen of the universe, he tells us that the image of an empty mirror—recall the title of his first volume—is his image for the defeat of visionary, metaphysical strivings. However, Ginsberg has not quit, in either his poetry or his life, to protest what he feels he ought, to point out what he considers to be wrong, to work for what he thinks is right. His opposition to the Vietnam War is well known. So is much of his other protest work. Very characteristic of his efforts was his active support of Norman Mailer and Jimmy Breslin in the New York City mayorality race of 1969. "They are to be congratulated for injecting character into politics,"[26] he said, and this is a clue to much of his philosophy. The character, the self, what he calls in one poem the "Me-ity" (*Planet*, p. 80) is where we are urged to turn for integrity of purpose—not to political systems, to language manipulators.

A writer for *Esquire* asked him about his future plans once and he responded, "To be real, that's what."[27] What is certainly included in this search to be real is a reliance on and a trust in feelings. Here again, Emerson (especially of "Self-Reliance") and Whitman (especially of *Leaves of Grass*) are Ginsberg's literary ancestors. Perhaps the reason is that in reacting emotionally, nothing is filtered through "Language language." Possibly even the poet, the great manipulator of language, and even when he is using obscenities at the unambiguous best, cannot ultimately trust in words. This is at least suggested in the work of Allen Ginsberg. It is certainly true of LeRoi Jones, the next poet we shall consider.

Notes and References

1. Allen Ginsberg, *Reality Sandwiches* (San Francisco, 1963), p. 40.

2. Edward C. Norton, "Louis Ginsberg & Son Poets," *Ave Maria*, CX (September 6, 1969), 27.

3. *College English*, XXVIII (March, 1967), 433.

4. "The Language of the Tribe," *Commonweal*, XC (22 August, 1969), 505.

5. Quoted in *Eldridge Cleaver* (New York, 1969), ed. by Robert Scheer in Mr. Scheer's Introduction, p. xxv.

6. Quoted in *The Beat Generation and the Angry Young Men*, ed. by Gene Feldman and Max Gartenberg (New York, 1958), p. 164.

7. Quoted in Paul Carroll, *The Poem in Its Skin* (Chicago, 1968), p. 83.

8. "Wichita Vortex Sutra" in *Planet News* (San Francisco, 1968), pp. 110-132.

9. Quoted in Jane Kramer, *Allen Ginsberg in America* (New York, 1968), p. 83.

10. *The New York Times Book Review* (December 28, 1969), pp. 1-2.

11. Ginsberg is not the first poet to be concerned about the development of language. Among moderns, Ezra Pound, William Carlos Williams, T. E. Hulme, and other imagists were equally troubled over the abuse of language. T. S. Eliot also addressed himself to the subject. For him it was, as Babette Deutsche says in her discus-

sion of Eliot, "The poet's ultimate problem, that of language" (*Poetry In Our Time* [New York, 1963], p. 165).

12. *The New American Poetry: 1945-1960*, ed. by Donald M. Allen (New York, 1960), p. 180.

13. *Ibid.*, p. 189.

14. *Planet*, p. 138.

15. *Sandwiches*, p. 24.

16. Allen Ginsberg, *Kaddish* (San Francisco, 1961), p. 61.

17. *Prayers* (New York, 1963), pp. 31-33.

18. *Look at Us, Lord* (Nashville, 1969).

19. Quoted in Carroll, p. 107.

20. Henry Thoreau, *Walden* (New York, 1964), p. 143.

21. "Walt Whitman and the Common Man," *American Dialog*, II (October-November, 1965), p. 10.

22. Quoted in *Writers at Work*, ed. by George Plimpton (New York, 1968), p. 306.

23. Quoted in Kramer, p. 159.

24. Bruce Hunsberger, "Kit Smart's Howl," *Wisconsin Studies in Contemporary Literature*, VI (Winter-Spring, 1965), 34-44.

25. See *Evergreen Review*, III (November-December, 1959), 132-135, for a fuller discussion.

26. Quoted in *Publisher's Weekly*, CXCV (June 23, 1969), 18.

27. Alice Glaser, "Back on the Open Road for Boys," *Esquire*, LX (July, 1963), 115.

V

Leroi Jones: The Poetry
of Exaggeration

IF ALLEN GINSBERG has changed the life sytle of a generation, LeRoi Jones expresses the life style of a significant segment of his contemporaries. Jones is the epitome of the militant, artistic black. Jones is not a writer who happens to have black skin. He sees himself not even as primarily militant. He is black. His acknowledgment of this is meant to tell us a great deal about him and his work.[1]

Jones is clearly an activist. What is disturbing to many literary critics, however, apart from his personal life, is the militant tone of Jones's creative work. His protest against a white society is found in his poetry, plays, and essays as well as in his life. He can write such lines as "Rape the white girls. Rape/ their fathers. Cut the mothers' throats."[2] In another poem we read; ". . . we must/ finally kill them [white men], rid the earth of them,/ because they are a diseased species. . . .[3] It is lines like these and dramas such as *Four Black Revolutionary Plays* (Indianapolis, 1969) that have led some to question Mr. Jones's integrity as an artist.[4] However, the judgments on Jones's work are usually hasty and fail to understand a tradition in which Jones is writing. Perhaps he himself would deny that he is in this tradition since he rather frequently makes derogatory or sarcastic remarks about other black artists. (He has been very critical of James Baldwin,[5] among others.) Yet there is a framework in which Jones operates and it must be recognized if his work is to be properly evaluated.

This framework is that of the tradition of oratory among black men in this country.[6] It was in the preaching in black churches that both the Christian faith and the broad history of black people were kept alive. The style of this black oratory was, in part, a style based on exaggeration. As Theodore Gross has written, "The significance of the church—and specifically the Protestant church—must be central to any discussion of Negro literature and its pervasive idealism, as it must be considered a formative influence on the development of transcendentalism. Equally significant in both types of writing is the deep impact of oratory on the written language."[7] Many people were surprised to hear Dr. Martin Luther King in television segments speak differently to an all black congregation than he did to a predominantly white audience. What these listeners failed to understand was that King was speaking to the blacks in the tradition of their oratory, a tradition of exaggeration that found its expression in jazz and other art forms—including writing. It would be absurd, for example, to believe that in *Native Son* Richard Wright was suggesting that every black man ought to kill a white woman. Ralph Ellison was not advocating race riots in *Invisible Man* and Chester Himes does not include violence in all of his novels simply because he loves violence. Their works are their expressions of the oratorical tradition.

Furthermore, when Eldridge Cleaver, Rap Brown, and Stokely Carmichael shout obscenities we need to look past the literal language to the meaning of the shock techniques being applied. Theirs may be, in a certain sense, an oratory gone wild. I think that this is equally true of LeRoi Jones's writing.

Jones is much like Ginsberg, a poet he sometimes

praises,[8] when Jones writes, "The language less than the act."[9] In the poem "If Into Love the Image Burdens" (*Lecturer*, p. 47) he makes the distinction between words and action, a distinction he can ultimately "perfect" in a wordless drama, "Resurrection in Life."[10] His most emphatic poem here is the twenty-one line "Young Soul" (*Magic*, p. 49).

All this, too, must be seen against a background that includes the tradition of exaggeration. Critics tend to remember most Jones's concern with violence. All of it is directed toward whitey. "I will slaughter/ the enemies/ of my father" (*Magic*, p. 197) Jones repeats twice in "From the Egyptian" and we can have no doubt who this enemy is. His *Four Black Revolutionary Plays* deals with killing the white man. *Experimental Death Unit #1* is about two white men destroyed while copulating with a black woman. These men are finally beheaded by black militants. In *A Black Mass* there is an African wise man who creates a vicious white beast (man). The drama ends when a black Narrator appears and says, "There are beasts in our world. Let us find them and slay them. Let us lock them in their caves. Let us declare the Holy War" (*Plays*, p. 39). "Kafkaesque" is perhaps the best descriptive word for *Great Goodness of Life*. A black man is brought to trial for a crime he cannot know he has committed. He is freed because "No one beautiful is guilty" (*Plays*, p. 59). He is forced to kill a murderer with a silver bullet to prove his worthiness, then is allowed to return to the everyday world.

Implicit here is a criticism of the non-beautiful, the white. There is also implicit criticism of this sort in *Madheart*, a morality play showing a black man proving his masculinity (stolen by society) through various violent acts including stabbing his "Uncle Tom" sister and beating a woman into submission. The author is correct in his "Introduction" to these plays when he tells us ungrammatically that "Unless you killing white people, killing the shit they've built, don't read this shit, you won't like it, and it sure won't like you" (*Plays*, p. vii).

The point that must be remembered in all of this, however, is made by Gross (p. 5): "And what is true of Negroes in general, of course, is intensified and often raised to a lyric cry or pugnacious propaganda in the literature of Negro authors." The following remarks by experts on black sociology have validity for black literature as well: "It would appear that throughout the history of American Negroes there has been a strong element of fantasy in Negro discussion and efforts concerning violent retaliation. . . . The Black Muslims talk of violence, but the talk functions as a psychological safety valve; by preaching separation they in effect accommodate to American social order and place racial warfare in the future when Allah in his time will destroy the whites and usher in an era of black ascendancy."[11] The notion of the "safety valve" may be applied to Jones's writing. True, "I am saying, now,/ what my father could not remember/ to say. What my grandfather/ was killed/ for believing" (*Magic*, p. 26) but the fact that he is saying it is healthy. He refuses to sing for his supper like his ancestors did. What Jones is exhibiting in his revolting poetry (ambiguity intended) is a race consciousness he is consciously trying to bring to bear on his work. "Look in your mother's head,/ if you really want to know everything" (*Magic*, p. 72).

There are the rather too labored passages in "Ka ' Ba" (*Magic*, p. 146) about the beautiful people with African imaginations and the entire correspondence of "our black family." Much more could be cited but these examples make the point. He looks at the white man and claims that his art "must hate them for hating" (*Home*, p. 211). Whether or not this is a humanely valid approach is not to be argued here. It is Jones's approach and we must recognize it. This approach is found in his art and in his writings on politics as well since for Jones the artist and the life he lives are not separable.

His consolation must be in his art and his activity, not in the work of others. His attack on what can be termed the "liberal establishment" bears this out:

> American liberals seem for the most part to fall out of a mold so fixed and predictable that they have become almost completely "neutralized" as far as the political life of this country is concerned. They have also developed into the most viciously wrong-headed group of amateur social theorists extant. They, or rather, you, liberals, are people with extremely heavy consciences and almost non-existent courage. Too little is always enough. And it is always the symbol, the token, that appeals to you most. For the Feiffer / Harrington / *Village Voice* liberal, the single futile housing project in a jungle of slums and disease eases your conscience, so you are loudest in praising it. The single black student in the Southern University, the promoted porter in Marietta, Georgia—all ease the liberal's conscience like a benevolent but highly addictive drug.
>
> (*Home*, p. 64)

What Jones says instead is that "the role of the black artist in America is to help in the destruction of America as it now exists. If what he does—whether it's polemical or lyrical or however it functions—if it contributes to that destruction, it is valid and finally beautiful."[13] In *The System of Dante's Hell* Jones has a chapter titled "(The Destruction of America" (p. 32). The unclosed parenthesis indicates what has become a favorite theme for Jones, the ongoing destruction of this nation.[14] However, destruction of America does not necessarily mean annihilation of this country. For Jones it means a re-ordering of values, instead. Jones emphasizes the evils so that they can become recognizable. Once obvious, they ought to be easily eliminated. Many militants want to wreck things, without a proposal for rebuilding. This is not true of Jones. In a letter to me, dated March 30, 1970, he invited me to assist his efforts toward representative government for minority groups in Newark, New Jersey. Here is one paragraph of that letter:

"We're asking you to support the candidates selected by the Black and Puerto Rican Convention by helping out with mailings, passing out leaflets, canvassing, etc., poll watching, whenever you can between now and election day May 12, 1970." This is not the letter of a violent man, nor was he writing to a supporter of violent action. Yet Margolies attacks Jones as one who "has transformed himself from a serious artist to a fiercely active nationalist, using his literary talents to effect what he regards as depending on one's point of view, but the fact is that much of Jones' recent writing has lost its depth and sensitivity while as propaganda it fails to arouse the violence Jones urges because, ironically, it is too erudite and subjective."[15]

If we can see Margolies' errors here, we will benefit a great deal in our understanding of Jones. That he is "too erudite" is misleading. Surely the audience to whom Jones is appealing comprehend the black poet very well. Even whitey can, if he gives Jones the necessary attention. Margolies' use of the term "subjective" in a pejorative sense does injustice to Jones. It is precisely the subjective nature of Jones's work that marks his protest as one of exaggeration rather than of literal value. In an early poem Jones says "Let my poems be a graph/ of me" (*Lecturer*, p. 10). But the graph is really a kind of published question mark in the active quest for identity, as Jones tries to answer the question each man must ask himself: Who am I? In fact, Jones spells it out in "Home": "But one truth anyone reading these pieces ought to get is the sense of movement —the struggle, in myself, to understand where and who I am, and to move with that understanding" (p. 9). "I write poetry to investigate my self, and my meaning and meanings" (*Magic*, p. 41). That is how we ought to read Jones, too. It is, in fact, what he is rather begging us to do. He almost pathetically wants us to notice him:

> It's so diffuse
> being alive. Suddenly one is aware
> that nobody really gives a damn.[16]

Come, give a damn, he says, "Among things with souls, find me" (*Magic*, p. 21).

> I am real, and I can't say who
> I am, Ask me if I know, I'll say
> yes, I might say no. Still, ask.
>
> (*Magic*, p. 47)

Don't just ignore me. Don't treat me like one of Ralph Ellison's invisible men. *Ask me!* Recognize my existence. Even hatred does that much.

Here is the big, tough, frightening revolutionary, acting like any of us:

> ... I am frightened
> that the flame of my sickness
> will burn off my face. And leave
> the bones, my stewed black skull,
> an empty cage of failure.
>
> (*Suicide*, p. 60)

Is this the subjectivism Margolies objects to? Jones's work is puerile at times, even whining on occasion; however, Margolies was not criticizing execution, but intention. This is at least an incomplete way to read any writer.

Part of our difficulty in accepting the overall protest that Jones is making is in his reliance on feeling over reason.[17] But as was indicated earlier, this is right in the midst of black tradition. That is why jazz has interested Jones and influences him so profoundly: "Negro music alone, because it drew its strengths and beauties out of the depth of the black man's soul, and because to a large extent its traditions could be carried on by the lowest classes of Negroes, has been able to survive the constant and willful dilutions of the black middle class" (*Home*, p. 106). In the same essay (p. 112) Jones says, "The most successful fiction of most Negro writing is in its emotional content." (In one of his earliest poems Jones referred to history as "A jungle/ of feeling." [Lecturer, p. 13].)

Apparently some see this as an automatically bad feature of Jones's work. I cannot agree. It has its dangerous elements, of course. Excess is one of those elements. George Dennison is right to criticize *The Slave* on the grounds that the whites in this play "are dummy figures and talk dummy language, but the language of the Negro revolutionary is frequently crackling and alive."[18] This is the kind of thing Jones will have to improve if he is to become a first-rate writer, a playwright and poet of unsuspect integrity.

It may be likely that Jones is not that concerned about his reputation, that he is trying to live up to the image that he has created of himself or that others have created of him, that he must be concerned only to help free his people from the shackles of a slavery that still persists. Must it then be a question of art or politics? Larry Neal thinks not: "The artist and the political activist are one. They are both shapers of the future reality. Both understand and manipulate the collective myths of the race. Both are warriors, priests, lovers and destroyers."[19] Writing in *The New York Times*, Jones agrees: "There is no such thing as Art and Politics, there is only life, and its many registrations."[20]

Daniel Berrigan, the Jesuit poet, would concur in this last remark. How differently he applies it, however, will be the subject of the final portion of this study.

Notes and References

1. Jones obviously agrees with Larry Neal's essay "And Shine Swam On" found in a book he and Neal edited, *Black Fire* (New York, 1968), in which we read that " . . . the black artist must link his work to the struggle for his liberation and the liberation of his brothers and sisters" (p. 655). As John Killens said of a seminar in which he, Jones and other black writers participated, "The question of whether the Negro writer or a writer who happens to be Negro has been settled for a long time. Most of the writers had no trouble knowing who they were. They knew they were Negro writers and they were proud of it." (For a discussion of this symposium see Nat Hentoff, "Uninventing the Negro," *Evergreen Review*, IX [November, 1965], 34-36, 66-69. The quotation is found on page 68.)

2. LeRoi Jones, *The Dead Lecturer* (New York, 1964), p. 63.

3. LeRoi Jones, *Black Magic* (Indianapolis, 1969), p. 99.

4. See, for example, Edward Margolies, *Native Sons* (Philadelphia, 1968), p. 194: "In recent years, Jones' anger has extended itself beyond his ability (or desire) to shape it artistically, and as a result his plays and poems have lost themselves in a kind of fretful hysteria."

5. See *Home* (New York, 1968), p. 117. "Joan of Arc of the cocktail party is what is being presented through the writings and postures of men like [Baldwin and Peter Abrahams, the South African writer]." In another essay in the same book, "A dark bag," Jones writes, " . . . part of every English sentence James Baldwin writes must be given over to telling a willing audience how sensitive and intelligent he is, in the face of terrible odds. Ralph Ellison's extra-literary commercial is usually about European literature, the fact that he has done some reading in it" (p. 123).

6. See my discussion of this in *National Catholic Reporter* (February, 1970), p. 16. The article is titled "What's Behind Black Rhetoric?"

7. "The Idealism of Negro Literature in America," *Phylon*, XXX (Spring, 1969), 6.

8. See Jones, *Magic*, p. 81.

9. Jones, *Lecturer*, p. 47. Perhaps one might argue as George Lamming does in "The Negro Writer and His World," *Cross Currents*, VI (Spring, 1956), 159, in speaking of the writer that "Language, it would seem, has actually surrendered just when his need is greatest." Allen Ginsberg would agree with Lamming and also make the remark applicable to all writers, not just black ones.

10. Of this unpublished play, Gerald Weales says, "It is a wordless fable, a pantomimed account of how the Beast (as in 'Black Mass,' Jones' designation for the white) stole knowledge, art, religion from the blacks and used the borrowed power to enslave the original discoverers. Enter, a black (consciousness?) who will not let himself be bullied by the white; the slaves are freed and the Beast returned to his cave." *The New York Times Magazine* (May 4, 1969), p. 58.

11. August E. Meier and Elliot M. Rudwick, *From Plantation to Ghetto* (New York, 1968), p. 250.

12. LeRoi Jones, *The System of Dante's Hell* (New York, 1965), p. 86.

13. Quoted in Hentoff, p. 35.

14. See Jones, *Magic*, p. i, where the author introduces this collection of three previous volumes of verse. He says of the third volume, *Target Study*, that it "is trying to really study, like bomber crews do the soon to be destroyed cities. Less passive now, less uselessly "literary.' "

15. Margolies, pp. 192-193.

16. Jones, *Preface to a Twenty Volume Suicide Note* ... (San Francisco, 1961), p. 15. For similar sentiments, see Jones's stories in *Tales* (New York, 1967), especially "Heroes Are Gang Leaders."

17. Ronald Berman, in *America in the Sixties* (New York, 1968), p. 109, says that "It is interesting to see that the real things Jones

dislikes are words like 'sensitivity,' 'reason,' 'respectability.' They are in his context all synonyms for thought."

18. *Commentary*, XXXIX (February, 1965), 68.

19. Jones and Neal, p. 656.

20. *The New York Times*, (November 16, 1969), p. 7.

VI

Daniel Berrigan: The Poet as Citizen

THERE IS a discernible trend blurring the distinction between art and life in the poets surveyed thus far. The distinction is strongest in Eberhart, weakest in Jones. In "Aesthetics After War" Eberhart was conscious of a division between aesthetics and living. He divided poetry into "Will poetry" and "Psyche poetry," which hints at a chasm between art and life. "Psyche poetry pertains to the soul, to peace, quiet, tranquility, serenity, harmony, stillness and silence. It provides psychic states of passive pleasure."[1] Eberhart's contrast follows: "Will poetry exists because of the power in the cell beyond its energy to maintain itself. Will results in action, through wish, zeal, volition, passion, determination, choice and command. Will makes something happen in poetry." The Rev. Daniel Berrigan, S.J., could take the above definitions and apply them not only to poetry, but to creative living as well; and whereas Eberhart does not indicate a preference for either of the two types of poetry he describes, there is no doubt which Berrigan would choose. There is no need to insist on one over the other, however; in Berrigan the conditions of passivity and action are fused. He is the contemplative who, in his reflection, is wound taut and then, because of what he has understood, springs forth in a torrent of disciplined activity—writing and acting.

Berrigan is the poet-citizen, citizen-poet. His living is as equally creative as is his writing. Larry Neal was quoted earlier as saying that "The artist and the political activist are one. They are both shapers of the future reality." Berrigan bears this out. His poetry has the intellectual base that Jones seems to lack. His work was publicly recognized in 1957 when he was awarded the Lamont Poetry Prize and again thirteen years later when he was nominated for the 1969 National Book Award in poetry. His life was "rewarded" with a three and a half year prison sentence for burning draft records as part of the Catonsville Nine on May 17, 1968.[2]

Daniel Berrigan was born May 9, 1921, in Virginia, Minnesota. He is the last of six boys born to Thomas and Frieda (Fromhart) Berrigan. The family moved to Syracuse and there Dan attended St. John the Baptist Academy. He entered the Society of Jesus on August 14, 1939, studied Thomistic philosophy at Woodstock College and theology at Weston College in Massachusetts, and was ordained a priest June 21, 1952. He studied further at the Gregorian University in Rome and at the Maison la Colombiere, Paray le Monial in France. Berrigan spent much of his time in France with people active in the Worker Priest Movement. In 1957 he began teaching theology at LeMoyne University in Syracuse where he was active in interracial groups. His first book of poetry was published in 1957. In 1964 Berrigan was appointed assistant editor of *Jesuit Missions* magazine, based in New York. He became active in the Catholic Worker movement, also with headquarters in New York and worked with other peace groups as well. Because of his outspoken opposition to the Vietnam war, he was sent to South America in November, 1965. This exile lasted three months and caused a great furor.[3] Some time after his return he was assigned to a chaplaincy at Cornell University. Berrigan participated in many protest activities crowning them with Catonsville. In that community, just outside of Baltimore, Berrigan and eight others invaded a draft board located in the Knights of Columbus Hall, took draft files outside, and burned them with homemade napalm. Dr. Robert McAfee Brown said of Catonsville: "I begin to think that that act may stand as the quintessential Christian act of our era, for it points up the grotesque reversal of priorities to which our age has succumbed, that we brand a man as criminal who drops napalm on paper, and acclaim another man as hero who drops napalm on children."[4] For this, the nine were sentenced to federal prison (including Dan's brother, the Rev. Philip Berrigan, S.J., a Servite priest). Dan was sentenced to three years in prison.

The destruction of draft files was never intended as a purely negative act. It was a demonstration of love, of support for life—not only the lives of U.S. soldiers but for the lives of the "enemy" as well, and the South Vietnamese too. This is the kind of act of love that Berrigan prepared for in his poetry. He could write, long before his involvement in any "movement," ". . . to learn not to love/ is the slavery."[5] More significantly, in a theological work, he said that by knowledge man enters creation, by love he assimilates it.[6] This is meaningful on several levels if we are to understand Berrigan properly. His notion of Incarnation is implied here, an idea we shall treat more fully later. "Which way is man"[7] he asks because he wishes to love him, to use the "password friend" (*Encounters*, p. 54). His love is the kind that will involve us, will blind us, will commit those of us who are the objects (or better, subjects) of it. "Allow me to love you. Pay the price. Love me."[8] This is a command written by a man certain of himself. Compare this to the more pitiful, less certain lines of LeRoi Jones in *Black Magic*: "Among things with souls, find me" (p. 21); or, "No single redeeming hand/ has ever been offered" (p. 23). Or, "I wd do anything/ to be loved" (p. 88). We must notice that Berrigan speaks of love in act: "It's what they heard His whole life say that counts" (*Love*, p. 110).

Implied is a sense of personal responsibility and this is a major theme in the works and life of Daniel Berrigan. He has been called one of those who "act as the conscience and memory for our generation."[9] Berrigan is not the subject of Karl Shapiro's poem "The Conscientious Objector," but certain of Shapiro's lines are applicable to him: "Your conscience is/ What we came back to in the armistice." Berrigan's ideas of personal responsibility are rooted in his understanding of Incarnational Theology. All of Berrigan's work has this foundation. In a review of his first book, *Time Without Number*, Sister M. Maura wrote in *Thought* of "the spirit of reverence toward creaturehood" in Berrigan's work and specifically indicated in his Incarnational approach.[10] Another reviewer said of this same book: "There is a reverence for life as an irrepeatable and irreplaceable gift, and the nervous presence of felt theological fact." Then follows the comment that in Berrigan's poetry, "One finds also a careful and articulate humanism of Incarnation."[11] Of *The Bow in the Clouds* a critic noted that "His book is an exploration of the truth that 'The Incarnation summons man to a new evaluation of his human life.'"[12] All of Berrigan's work has, as Etta May Van Tassel said of *Encounters*, "That contemplative vision of reality."[13] Berrigan, in a conversation we had, speaks of his writing as becoming increasingly Incarnational. In our talk he insisted on the recognition of the value of this world, of the "here and now." There is an acceptance of reality implicit in Berrigan's early poetry which is rendered explicitly in his later work. The contrast can be seen in a poem from each period. "As Rational As Human" appears in *Time Without Number* (p. 25) and even its irony implies an acceptance of the world:

> Only mid-September: already the doomed
> earnest little dancer, the maple, is a cloak of flame.
> On tiptoe, here and there, in and out of the pine groves,
> he mimes and whirls.

> But the pines ho-hum and yawn
> into every wind. They have been there, they will be
>   there
> so long, so long, stomping huge feet in the cold,
> blinking and disbelieving the miraculous spring sun.
>
> Why then attend or sympathize the doomed
> attentive little dancer, shod in cursed slippers,
> cloaked in absolute fire, dancing his careful ruinous
> geometrics about them?
>   In a few days, the legend goes,
> his flame will out: but time will vindicate them
> as rational, as human, who welcomed reality with care
>
> a needful distance from its pernicious fires.

In *False Gods, Real Men*, published in 1969, nearly a dozen years after *Time Without Number*, Berrigan's work is more explicitly Incarnational and affirmative. Here is "Tree":

> Botched together
> a board fence
> a neanderthal mockup
>
> Suddenly something
> occurred,
> ball to socket to
> skull, I stood up
>
> stood like a self willed savior
> grinning, baiting big bad death
>
> clutching my hornbook
> crying to mother earth; I am!

> (p. 92)

Examples need not be multiplied. Berrigan is an Incarnationalist. One of the effects of his Incarnationalism is a concreteness of imagery and subject matter. For Berrigan this has meant an approach that is consciously simple. He feels that a man's task is to simplify where possible. He is disturbed when people complicate issues.

A consciously simple approach results in simple language in Berrigan's poems. John Logan challenged Berrigan to write poems without using certain common words over and over again, words like "heart" and "death."[14] Logan has missed, I think, how much Berrigan's work is rooted in the ordinary, the real. For James Joyce art "is the human disposition of sensible or intelligible matter for an aesthetic end."[15] This is not so for Berrigan (or for LeRoi Jones). It is indeed the opposite for Berrigan. The ends must be fully human, fully Incarnational. Again, for Berrigan, Incarnational somehow means simplifying. This places him squarely in the pastoral tradition as discussed by Leo Marx in *The Machine in the Garden*. Marx writes of pastoralism as still being a significant force in American life and letters: the pastoralism of Thoreau, Melville, Twain, Frost, and others. However, as his title indicates, the garden has been invaded by technology. Industrialism is a counterforce to the pastoral design.[16] This counterforce is precisely what we find in Berrigan's later poetry. Berrigan recognizes this when he says that in *False Gods, Real Men* he introduces technology in the form of war. "The way I translate my attitude is to confront the machine with a Man,"[17] he told me in a personal interview. Another way of saying this is to say that the world is confronted by the author. Berrigan admits to this because "we've passed into a notion of time as crisis. And not a crisis 'out there,' but a crisis in here, generated by out there. So that the world and our own consciousness are constantly trying one another out."

One result of this confrontation between Berrigan and the world is a political theology. It is welded to his Incarnationalism as well as his concept of poetry as an adjunct of creative living. Jackson J. Benson recognized how bound up art and life are with each other when he observed this about Ernest Hemingway: "The writer of our time, be he novelist, poet, or playwright, seems to have found the problems of art and the problems of living to be more crucially joined together as aspects of the same problem than did most of his predecessors."[18] It is seen more clearly, more positively, by Gardner Murphy in his vastly influential work, *Human Potentialities*: "Creativeness can transcend an art form and become a quality of life."[19] What Berrigan has done, others did before him. He has fused his approach to politics and poetry in the sense that Dante did.

Berrigan's, like the Dantesque view, is a thoroughly Christian one. In a work titled "Sacred Art and the Life of Man,"[20] Berrigan is concerned with art as manifest spirituality. Quotations will indicate what I mean here, but it should be kept in mind that, perhaps even unbeknown to the author, he is speaking of what is to be seen as his own art—in poetry and in "secular" act. In speaking of art in previous ages Berrigan says, "The Christian would radiate in his world the holy energies that lay powerfully within the Christian mysteries and their expression—energies that awaited release through faith, worship, and sacrificial love" (p. 90). He next discusses the basilica apse as powerful setting for "dramatizing the Mass in art" (pp. 90-91) particularly emphasizing the Church militant. "Christian life in this world honored human realities; indeed, it was built up of them" (p. 91). On the same page we read that the Catholic Church set the images of her great men in the sanctuaries because the Church wished to warn the faithful against the Gnostic sense of eternity—a separatist sense which asks believers to "pass through this world with sterile hands and minds." Acknowledgment of reality implies a maturing of the individual, a recognition of God's world and man's mission in it. Art can assist in this maturation. It can also hinder it if it is of the plastic statue variety of Jesus found on automobile dashboards. Weak, "comforting" art is made of images that "strike one as a massive form of resistance against the threat and demands of maturity" (p. 95). And a few lines later: "They allow no suspicion to reach man that Christianity is a matter of deeds, even of one's blood." This is "visual heresy" (p. 99) to Berrigan who would hold that true creativity is today true asceticism, true holiness, true sacrifice, true love. Here we have the poet as prophet.[21] Berrigan is very consistent in his approach. It is as if all of his works, while individual pieces, were part of a great mosaic giving the meaning of his existence as he understands it. This is remarkable if we remember that Berrigan's writing covers a span that begins long before the Vietnam war, long before his participation in anti-segregation demonstrations. He could write, "The greatness of art; it cries *reality*!"[22] He can see the poem as "the journey toward" (*Waters*, p. 44). The focus, it must be repeated, is on the work to be done in this life: "The aim of great ideas or great art or great policy, is incarnation, embodiment, a new man, a new form, a new community."[23]

One obstacle, among others, that Berrigan sees to "successful incarnation" (my phrase) is another kind of soft art, the abuse of language. Allen Ginsberg and LeRoi Jones were outspoken in their linguistic treatment of the subject, and Berrigan would support them. "The obscenity of the sons is purer than the hypocrisy of the parents," he writes in his fourteenth book (*No Bars*, p. 70). This becomes clearer when we read, earlier on that page, "Obscene. A major portion of public speech, embracing as it does death for its method, recommending destruction and division as invaluable social tools, is in the strictest classical sense, obscene speech." He writes of this seducing speech and then strongly insists that "the gospel language condemns our usual language. . . ." All of this occurred not long after he noted that the President took his oath of office on a biblical passage that spoke of exchanging weapons for tools. He notes the projected increase in annual military budgets, and laments that "I am concerned with so simple a thing as language" (*No Bars*, p. 67). For illustration, he follows with simple scriptural passages about peace, hypocrisy, and perhaps most telling of all, "Let your words be simply yea and nay." Years before he had said,

> Angry in his shift of blood
> Christ cannot die, so many soft tongues breathe
> false comfort to his wounds.[24]

Some critics find the power of Berrigan the poet in his spareness, his integrity.[25] What they tend to overlook, however, is a quality in Berrigan's work which is akin to that of LeRoi Jones: exaggeration. This is evident in his conversation: "Let the bishops play the corporation game, let them indulge in the worst sacred rhetoric to conceal their real selves from themselves." Exaggeration is also obvious in his writing: To be a black student at Cornell "could not be a different thing from being a black in the gold mines of Johannesburg, or a Congolese at the mercy of white man's guns, or a Venezuelan oil worker cursed with the vocation to enrich the Rockefellers" (*No Bars*, p. 198). Only John Leonard, so far as I have been able to determine, has scolded Berrigan for what might be termed linguistic excesses. He calls Berrigan's words on Cornell "preposterous."[26]

Daniel Berrigan's most profound "fully human" expression of his understanding of his own participation in the Incarnation of Christ took place on May 17, 1968, at Catonsville where he destroyed draft files with his brother Phillip, the late Brother David Darst, former student at St. Louis University, Thomas Melville a former Maryknoll priest and his wife Marjorie, a former nun of that order, George Mische who had worked for the State Department, John Hogan an ex-Maryknoll brother, Mary Moylan, a nurse, and artist Thomas Lewis. They exemplified, to their own satisfaction at least, what Berrigan had written in a poem about a decade before:

Truest credo is event, would say
and said it to a brother's face

(*Wedding Ring*, p. 5)

There is a danger implicit in the poet's attitude that must not go unrecognized. Demogogues, too, put belief into action. Hitler thought he was right. So do many of the people prosecuting the Vietnam war, the very fact against which the Catonsville incident was aimed. What we must say for Berrigan is this: he at least has the humility to admit that his position may not be without blame. In our interview he noted that "Even though we may be wrong, where we are is right. I'm not interested in this or that issue being right. I'm interested in being in the right place when Christ returns." A point to be made here is that the act of Catonsville may well be the culmination of the direction that the protest poets we have discussed previously have been going. In "Aesthetics after War," as we saw earlier, Richard Eberhart spoke of poetry in Western civilization never being able to escape intrusive action. This was just preliminary to later poets being able to say that poetry and action ("life") are no longer separate categories for the poet. Robert Lowell registered his witness by being a conscientious objector to a war. Allen Ginsberg's many utterances of protest, his participation in demonstrations up to and including the now famous trial of the Chicago Seven all show him as a man in the tradition marked by Berrigan's words, "truest credo is event. . . ." LeRoi Jones is likewise treading the same path which, while it cannot be said to be a worn one, is certainly a recognizable one along which others can be expected to walk.

To say that Berrigan puts belief into action, however, is not to exhaust Berrigan's notions of art or of life. For him, "Creation is summons." To be born is to be called. To create is to call. For the artist-man, conscious of his full humanity, the responsibility is to call on oneself and the accompanying responsibility is to answer this summons.

Merely to exist is to be in danger of parisitism. Not everyone will agree that Berrigan's words or his acts are virtuous, but it seems unlikely that he will be judged as lukewarm. He is not a part of a silent generation, a silent majority (or minority). Some fear the danger of lawlessness and anarchy which might result if each individual follows his own conscience in acting contrary to the civil laws of the country. However, Berrigan lives in a time when utter conformity is a frightening danger; when politicians and ideals as well as products are being marketed to a consumer public whose resistance levels are known with almost scientific precision. (See Joe McGinness' *The Selling of the President*, New York, 1969.) For Berrigan, sucking the world is sinful, feeding it is virtuous. "Come passionately into life" (*Waters*, p. 70) Berrigan says, echoing Eberhart's thoughts on living at a pitch near madness. Lowell's plea for sanity is likewise recalled. Ginsberg hoped for a holy madness which would reveal the madness of men's ways. All of this is summed up in Berrigan's insistence on passionate living. "Does man live only in thought?" Berrigan asks and answers with another question: "Where are his hands?" (*Waters*, p. 64). It is not to be forgotten that one of his books of poems is titled *Encounters*.

The early Christian was an activist and this is not lost on Berrigan (see *Dead Men*, p. 122). His repeated praise for St. Paul contains the idea of Paul's "apostleship" in this sense.[27] To be active is to carry a cross, to suffer or at least be willing to suffer. Berrigan worries that for those of us with suburban mentalities, too often the choices we allow ourselves involve the comfortable, the easy (*Dead Men*, p. 122).

What all of this implies, of course, is an interest in the events of this life, of an Incarnational view of the world. For Berrigan, the problem of man's work in the world is best represented in the struggle of the just man for peace, the man who will not pay the ultimately disrespectful act to another human being, the killing or condoning of killing in war. To be "forced to kill" is to lose control over a situation, and man is summoned to control. "Man knows, even obscurely, that he is called to create the world, which is both outside him and within him. He cannot evade his dominion over creation without destroying himself" (*Dead Men*, p. 159). The reason is, as he cites in the next paragraph, "Man and the world form a moral unity." Man simply cannot evade his responsibilities to the world unless he is willing to commit suicide. Yet he is in danger of doing just that: "Peacemaking, which is the profound and first issue of modern times and the first capacity of healthy men, is no longer seen as spiritual power, capable of bringing violence under the control of reason. The work of peace no longer belongs in any true sense to the people—to the artists, the philosophers, the historians, to those men whose disciplines have given them important, even irreplaceable insights into the meaning of man and his society" (*Dead Men*, p. 167). On the next page Berrigan insists that "We cannot retreat to the theological barricades. . . . The world can be healed, as the Bible makes clear, only by those who take its own flesh." Nor must men of good will wait for the churches to lead them. The poetry we are talking about in these pages is anti-establishment poetry and for many, as for Berrigan, the churches are a part of the establishment. (Ginsberg, it will be remembered, called the Vietnam conflict a chancery war.) Berrigan writes "The Chanceries and Pentagons can concoct a rhetoric to justify our murders."[28] In a time of crisis, the Church had waited on the culture[29] Berrigan lamented. He also insists that religion in the service of war is debasing.[30]

Berrigan demands more than mere passive objection to war, either on the part of churches or on the part of individuals. His is "a compelling call to engagement."[31] "I caused Christ sorrow" says the poet in *Encounters* (p. 71) and after this recognition, the constant call to action is heard. He is the man of whom Richard Eberhart speaks in "The Protagonist" when he says:

But I see a man in blue denim, walking
Through the halls of conscientious objection,
Because he took Christ seriously, immured.
A literalist of the imagination! who
Believed do unto others—Thou shalt not kill!

(*CP*, p. 181)

It is his Christian literalness that motivates Berrigan. The Christian intellectual, he has said, "accepts as his task the restoration of an atmosphere of life in which the claims of the faith may win a hearing. The task rightly understood is a public one and an intellectual one."[32] The task seems to be this: understand the job that has to be done—then work to give this understanding a hearing.

Berrigan attempts to achieve this through personal sacrifice.[33] Concerning life, he writes,

be yourself mercilessly
be serious in the world   uncorrupted by our gods
stand unwavering
beside the faulty and perplexed
the ridden and victimized
speak modestly   act audaciously
sing FREEDOM in the teeth of law

(*Love*, p. 88)

This is the equivalent of what he asked of himself as a poet early in his writing career:

Color it not kind
with skies of love and amber:
make it plain with death
and bitter as remember.

(*Time*, p. 4)

Much later he echoed both of the above emphatically in *Night Flight to Hanoi* (p. 21):

> I touch
> shrapnel and flesh, and risk my reason
> for truth's sake . . .

What worries this poet-citizen is our "normalcy" during
war. Are men aware of what is really happening? If they
are not, it is because they are somehow removed from the
action. Whether Berrigan would blame a suburban state of
mind, a military-industrial complex, a decline in moral
values or a combination of these and other causes (as
indeed he does) is not the point. He does remind us,
though, that bomber pilots are "proxies/ for all provi-
dence" (*False Gods*, p. 21) just as he told us earlier in
prose of "The biography of the white Westerner. He re-
quires (1) someone to kill for him and (2) someone to die
for him. His power is such that he can arrange both re-
quirements, that of vicarious executioner and vicarious
corpse" (*Night Flight*, p. 27).

This Western white is failing to concentrate on the development of the "I." He cannot comprehend what the poet
is trying to tell him about existence in these two lines:

> I am never complete, history
> awaiting its further emblem.

> (*False Gods*, p. 69)

Each of us is the "now" of history, and Berrigan, as I read
him, is saying that we are the culminating point of the past
and the beginning point for the future. This is not obvious
to all men, so Berrigan, in an almost prophetic role, lays
blame. He shames the clergyman who neglects the needy
while

> blessing fat publicans, their pockets
> where he fleeces.[34]

Hyperbolic as those lines are, they seem the tone of an
ordained Eberhart who, as indicated earlier, is willing to

accuse all of mankind when it comes to problems such as war. It is the question James O'Gara asked when he wrote that while he did not sympathize with all of the activities of the Berrigan brothers, he could appreciate the conscience-jogging in which they were engaged. O'Gara writes of some of the atrocities of World War II and asks "where were the Bishops and theologians and just plain Catholics then?"[35] This is the climate of the discussion Berrigan has aimed to foster in his poetry and his life. His response has been an uncomplicated one. "No man today could claim the right of dying on the terrain he was born into, can sign a covenant binding him to the past, to privileges, possessions, nation or color."[36] A man works for change, if he is fully man. "One is simultaneously subject to change and yet must bring change about."[37] This is understood and encouraged, even at the risk involved, both to his personal freedom and to his writing.[38] Francine du Plessix Gray in her article on the Berrigan brothers in the *New Yorker* alludes to both the change and the risk in the following passage on Daniel Berrigan: "His trips behind the Iron Curtain confirmed him in what is known as the theology of Kenosis, which had germinated in the French avant-garde of the forties. The believers in kenosis—the Greek work for 'emptying out,' which St. Paul used when he asked the Philippians to strip themselves of worldly ambitions, as Christ humbled himself in becoming man—ask the Church to strip itself of all material wealth and power. According to many adherents of this theology of poverty, the truest Christians are the ones who are poor and persecuted, who make no obeisance to secular power, who live in a community of risk . . ." (p. 70).

Any human risk has to be carried out in time. It is time, not eternity, where salvation will be achieved for the Christian. Of the poets discussed in this work, none has a greater sense of the urgency of time than Berrigan has. Eberhart and Ginsberg do not seem to have a great deal to say about the subject of time. Shapiro sees it as a corrupting influence. Time is the framework of culture, and culture is to be escaped if one is to remain innocent. Shapiro uses poetry as a means to remain innocent, which is a Christian-Freudian understanding of time. Christ urged his followers to become as little children, while Freud insisted that innocence is found in childhood and man's quest for guilt-free existence will be ended satisfactorily when man somehow returns to the innocence of childhood.

Shapiro continually works toward this return. Lowell sees time at least as a connecting link with the past. Not to know the past is not to know ourselves, not to understand from whence we came and thus to have no idea where we are going. Jones refers to time only in the sense that history is on his side. I have heard Stokely Carmichael say that the wheels of history grind for the black militants and I am convinced that Jones feels this also. But for Daniel Berrigan, time is much more an explicit theme than in Eberhart, Shapiro, Lowell, Ginsberg, or Jones. The Pentecost is the opposite of Nirvana. It is, in fact, ecstasy in time (*Bow*, p. 111). Time neglected, then, cancels eternity (*Wedding Ring*, p. 72). For the Christian, for the Incarnationalist, this is akin to the greatest individual tragedy. Bloy said that the only tragedy is not to be a saint.[39] Berrigan would say that sanctity is achieved by our efforts in this world, not in praying for the next world. Man's task is to redeem the evil of the times (Gray, p. 108). In an interview previously noted Berrigan says that a student will want the one indispensable start that theology and philosophy can give him. When the interviewer asked if this was toward eternity, Berrigan answered, "No, it is a start within time. It is a start within the city of men."[40] Certainly for an Incarnationalist, time has this value. No doubt he does see with Lowell that the more man immerses himself in history, the more he can see the pattern of history (see *Bride* p. 29). Time also acts as a judgment on man's works in this world. Berrigan tells us in *The Bride* (p. 48) that human work which endures bears on it the stamp of judgment that time sifts. This is more poetically rendered in the second poem of Berrigan's first collection, *Time Without Number.* "The Crucifix" tells about a cross at a Quebec roadside. Time has washed away the features of this religious symbol, but this has acted to make its true meaning more obvious. In my interview with Berrigan he indicates that he sees time as crisis. He says that our sense of time is relational, that we keep struggling with the alternatives that we can offer death. This then leads us to the last category in Berrigan's work that bears examining here, the subject of death.

It would seem that a specifically Christian poet, an Incarnationalist who understands time as providing the opportunity for salvation, would have an optimistic view concerning death. If there is any proper Christian view of death it ought to be one of hope.[41] But this is not the case with Berrigan. In my interview with him Berrigan is very pessimistic about life and death in both words and tone. It is almost surprising to see an activist without a great deal of hope. It is as if Berrigan is now reacting to conditions rather than confident of changing them.

This is not new in Berrigan. It is not accurate to say that his pessimism stems from his persecution and prosecution by church and state. In a review of *No One Walks Waters*, published almost exactly two years before Catonsville, Joseph Wilson wrote that "Berrigan's attempts at optimism are generally unconvincing."[42] I agree. He could write of Christ:

> He leaped eternity
> the whisper goes, a tiger to its prey.[43]

In this poem, "Death Casts No Light on the Mind," the tone is joyful. Berrigan can also sing rather abstractly of the happiness of resurrection, as in the following poem simply titled "Song":

The mind's life I sing, the subtle unageing humor
that poured in nostril and ear, raises the dead.
The heart's life, whose symbol is cormorant, hart.
Imagination that shakes the tame world
as thought grows blooded and particular

So after death, the clear eyes of existence
like a forest burning foxes fed on,
a plain of shins and thighs
a word could leaf out, and would, green again.

(Wedding Ring, p. 22)

In his first book of poems he saw only death as a savior (*Time*, p. 18). But in his next book, *Encounters*, he writes of growth as death laid on youth. In a more recent book death is portrayed as taking on the bishops' role and the parallel here is flattering to neither physical annihilation nor episcopacy (*Love*, pp. 10-11). The words "die" and "death" appear an enormous number of times throughout Berrigan's work. Paradoxically, he told me that his own death "doesn't terribly interest me." Astonishing as this may seem in a poet whose works speak a great deal about death, it seems true. In his earlier works, it is abstract death about which Berrigan writes. Later, it is the death of humans, particularly through war, that concerns him. He does not wonder what it would be like to be dead nor does he lament the cruel sentence of death which hangs over every man.

Richard Eberhart wrote much about death and we noted earlier Ralph Mills's observation that mortality was one of the three great themes in Eberhart's work. Robert Lowell's "death wish" in his work has also been alluded to earlier. Karl Shapiro, Allen Ginsberg, and LeRoi Jones also treat of the subject, from several perspectives of course. When we reflect on all of the poets covered in this work, we can see how generally joyless they are. This is particularly surprising in men like Jones, who would seem to intellectualize that history is on his side; like the Lowell of the autobiographically "Catholic" period and like the Shapiro of the similar time in his life; like the Nirvana-seeking Ginsberg. However, Lowell finds no joy or comfort in Christianity, Ginsberg despairs, Jones has an anger that may not be rooted in hope, Shapiro's irony cannot signify hope and Berrigan's poetry, at least in relation to the subject of death, is not Catholic poetry at all. In prose he could say that "Where there was no joy, hope must suffice" (*Love*, p. 46). But in poetry:

> No Recourse. The case of Jesus Christ
> is closed. Make what you will
> desire, regret, he lies
> stigmatized, a broken God
> the world had sport of.
> Risen? we have not turned that page.
>
> (*False Gods*, p. 71)

When in jail he would pen:

> FAITH, HOPE, LOVE ITSELF
> WAS A GREAT LIE.[44]

So here is Daniel Berrigan, the man-poet, the culmination, at least in the "now," of some of the major themes of some the major anti-establishment American poets of our time, a sad man, beaten as of May, 1970, the month he was to go to prison. Yet our conclusion must not be so pessimistic from a Berrigan point of view. St. Paul and St. John of the Cross wrote very hopeful things while in prison. Many others have also. As for happiness, it is not the artist's role to communicate joy, but to communicate his insights. In the crucial years we are experiencing, a thinker whose message was somehow joyful must be either suspect or must face the charge of not being relevant. At least in the course of relevancy, Daniel Berrigan cannot receive a failing grade.

Notes and References

1. Quote in Ralph Mills, Jr., *Richard Eberhart* (Minneapolis, 1966), p. 34.

2. In "Acts of Witness," by Francine du Plessix Gray. *The New Yorker*, March 14, 1970, p. 50, Berrigan is quoted as listing his awards and honors at the request of a publisher this way: "Lamont Poetry Award, 1957. Indictment, 4 felonies, U.S. Government, May 1968: Conspiracy, Entering Government property, etc., etc."

3. Berrigan's own brief account of his exile and the public's reaction to it is in *No Bars to Manhood* (New York, 1970), p. 21.

4. *Commonweal*, LXXXIX (December 6, 1968), 356. For an account of the participants' attitudes concerning Catonsville, see Berrigan's play based on the court proceedings: *The Trial of the Catonsville Nine* (Boston, 1970).

5. *Time Without Number* (New York, 1957), p. 29.

6. *The Bride* (New York, 1959), p. 33.

7. *Encounters* (Cleveland, 1960), p. 49.

8. *Love, Love at the End* (New York, 1968), p. 19.

9. Sam A. Eisenstein, "For Dan Berrigan, S.J.—Love, in Cuffs," *The National Catholic Reporter*, December 18, 1968, p. 5.

10. *Thought*, XXXIII (Summer, 1958), 279.

11. Thomas Coffey, "A New Light on Catholic Letters," *Spiritual Life*, IV (March, 1958), 10. See also the review of *Time Without Number* by Joseph P. Clancy, *Spirit*, XXIV (November, 1957), 145-147.

12. Anonymous review in *The Wiseman Review*, CCXXXVI (Winter, 1962), 356.

13. "Vision of Reality," *Spirit*, XXVII (May, 1960), 57.

14. "Poetry Shelf," *The Critic*, XXI (April-May, 1963), 85.

15. *A Portrait of the Artist as a Young Man* in *The Essential James Joyce*, edited by Harry Levin (London, 1948), p. 330.

16. *The Machine in the Garden*, p. 27.

17. Agreement with much of the foregoing may be found in the Raymond Benoit's discussion of contemporary work in "The New American Poetry," *Thought*, XLIV (June, 1969), 201-218. He says that "Sanctity is not a matter of other worldliness; the poet anchors it in this world with a decisively powerful particularity" (p. 209). He also discusses certain contemporary poets in relation to the pastoral tradition in American literature.

18. *Hemingway* (Minneapolis, 1969), p. 189.

19. *Human Potentialities* (New York, 1958), p. 141.

20. *They Call Us Dead Men* (New York, 1966), pp. 89-101.

21. Cf. *Unity* (September, 1968), p. 2, and *Ave Maria* LXXXXVII (19 January, 1963), 28, for examples of critics who agree.

22. *No One Walks Waters* (New York, 1966), p. 2.

23. *Consequences: Truth and ...* (New York, 1967), p. 5.

24. *The World for Wedding Ring* (New York, 1962), p. 75.

25. This is true of Ralph Mills, Jr., who finds Berrigan a new Hopkins, a continuation of Eberhart and Lowell in "Three Younger Poets," *Poetry*, CIX (November, 1966), 116. Others who support this position include Phyllis McGinley, "Beep, Beep," *America*, XCIX (26 October, 1957), 110-111; Thomas P. McDonnell, "A Part Apart," *Renascence*, XI (Spring, 1959), 166; Anthony Vader, review of *Time Without Number*, *The Critic*, XVI (December, 1957), 34; A. M. Sullivan, review of *Time*, *Catholic World*, CLXXXVI (January, 1958), 317.

26. *The New York Times*, April 1, 1970, p. 43.

27. For Berrigan on St. Paul, for example, see *Dead Men*, pp. 121-155, and *No Bars*, pp. 109-116.

28. *Night Flight to Hanoi*, (New York, 1968), p. 27.

29. "The Embattled Conscience," *Continuum*, VI (Summer, 1968), 118.

30. "Fidelity to the Living IV: Reflections," *Continuum*, V (Spring, 1966), 118.

31. See Michael Christopher, "Three Approaches to Involvement," *U.S. Catholic*, XXXII (May, 1966), 63, where the author comments on Berrigan's *They Call Us Dead Men*.

32. *The Bow in the Clouds* (New York, 1961), p. 200.

33. See John Mahoney on *The Bride* in *Ave Maria*, XC (8 August, 1959), 163-166.

34. Berrigan, *Wedding Ring*, p. 74. Berrigan can praise clerics, too, however. See *Wedding Ring* p. 43, and again p. 74, for example.

35. "Men of Peace," *Commonweal*, LCCCI (19 March, 1965), 779.

36. "Reflections on the Priest as Peacemaker," *Jubilee*, XIII (February, 1966), 29.

37. Berrigan, *Consequences*, p. 5. Berrigan understands, however, that change for its own sake is dangerous. One sentence after the above quotation we read, "Certain things will always endure, if change is not to become chaos."

38. Maureen Sullivan wrote of *Love, Love at the End* that "it's true that with this book the author has probably left behind more readers than lie in his future—a choice he can hardly be unaware of." *Jubilee*, XIII (February, 1966), 22-23.

39. See also Albert Camus, *The Plague* (New York, 1948), pp. 230-231. The character Tarrou speaks: "Can one be a saint without God?—that's the problem, in fact the only problem, I'm up against today."

40. Coffey, "A Talk," p. 315.

41. See *Death and Hope*, edited by Harry J. Cargas and Ann White, S.L. (Cleveland, 1970).

42. *Ave Maria*, CIII (14 May, 1966), 8.

43. Berrigan, *Wedding Ring*, p. 55. See also p. 64.

44. Daniel Berrigan, and Thomas Lewis, *Trial Poems* (Boston, 1970), last page. (Volume is unpaginated.)

Index

Index

Index